THE ATLANTIC CRITICAL REVIEW

QUARTERLY

APRIL – JUNE 2007

VOLUME 6 NUMBER 2

ATLANTIC

PUBLISHERS & DISTRIBUTORS (P) LTD

CONTRIBUTORS

Ioana Sasu-Bolba, University "Babeş-Bolyai", Cluj-Napoca, Faculty of Letters, Romania.

Ajoy Sengupta, Lecturer in English, Purulia College. [R] Shanti Apartment (Opp. Indian Bank) Apcar Garden (East), Asansol-4, Dist. Bardhaman, West Bengal.

Behzad Pourgharib, Research Scholar, Department of English, University of Mysore, Mysore. [R] Door No. 816/A, Ground Floor, Third Stage, Gokulum, Mysore, Karnataka.

Pilar Sánchez Calle, Departmento de Filologia Inglesa, facultad de Humanidades y CC.CC.de la Educación, University of Jaén, Jaén, Spain.

Hem Sharma Paudel, Lecturer, Central Department of English, Tribhuvan University, Kirtipur, Kathmandu.

Mallikarjun Patil, Reader, Department of English, Gulbarga University, Gulbarga, Karnataka.

Chaitali Gorai, Research Scholar, Department of English, Burdwan University, Burdwan. [R] C/o Sri Rama Prasad Garai, Nehru Road, Taldanga, PO. Chirkunda, Dist. Dhanbad.

Ujjwal Jana, Lecturer, Department of English, Bajkul Milani Mahavidyalaya, Purba Medinipur, PO. Kismat-Bajkul, West Bengal.

Anuradha Singh, Lecturer in English, Gopaldas Hindu Girls' College, Moradabad, U.P. [R] 58 A, Civil Lines, Moradabad, U.P.

Bhagabat Nayak, Lecturer in English, Kandarpur College, Cuttack, Orissa.

Devika, Lecturer, Languages Group, BITS Pilani, Rajasthan.

THE ATLANTIC CRITICAL REVIEW
VOLUME 6 NUMBER 2 (APRIL-JUNE 2007)

CONTENTS

William Blake's Teachings

IOANA SASU-BOLBA

MUCH has been said both about William Blake the man and William Blake the artist, and not seldom the remarks concerning him were rather malicious. Nevertheless, he remains one of the greatest poets and a strange one at that. But who is in fact the person who has been so often remembered and mentioned as the "visionary" poet?

William Blake is an English poet, visionary mystic, painter, and engraver who can be said to be unique. He is unique in the same way Shakespeare, Milton, Spenser, or Yeats are unique, that is to say they couldn't have been imitated, had no direct or successful disciples, did not form a literary school, etc. They all belong to a group of *timeless* and *spaceless* writers, mostly concerned with seeking existential Truths, digging into the human soul in order to find the *essential*, the very *reason of living* there.

He was born November 28, 1757, in Golden Square, London, being one of the five children of the family. His father, James, was a successful hosier attracted by the doctrines of Emmanuel Swedenborg[1], but could only afford to give William enough schooling to learn the basics of reading and writing.[2] Although he received little formal schooling, he kept reading the Bible, Milton, Greek and Latin classic literature throughout his life. His mother was the one in charge of his education. However, his mother seems to have been especially supportive. She even kept in her room some of William's drawings. His intellectual and psychological growth was dominated by the influence of his brother Robert, who died of consumption at the age of 20.[3] Although William was not bent to reading, it soon became quite clear that he was powerfully attracted by drawing. Therefore, he attended for a short time a drawing school run by Henry Par.

On the 4 August 1772, Blake became apprenticed to an engraver, James Basire, for seven years. At the end of that period he had become a professional engraver. Gothic art and architecture influenced him deeply. He sent Blake to Westminster Abbey to copy images of sculptures and from tombs. There were Blake's experiences in Westminster Abbey that first informed his artistic ideas and style. The Abbey offered a different environment: it was decorated with suits of armour, painted funereal effigies and varicoloured waxworks.

In 1779, Blake became a student at the Royal Academy, near the Strand. There he rebelled against painters like Rubens, whom he considered as having an unfinished style and against the school's first president, Joshua Reynolds who was in pursuit of "general truths." Blake responded by saying: "to generalise is to be an idiot; to particularise is alone the distinction of merit."[4]

In 1782 Blake met John Flaxman, who was to become his patron. In the same year, after having passed through a sentimental deception, he met, in the countryside, Catherine Boucher, the daughter of a market gardener, whom he married the following year. They had a happy marriage of about 45 years. Catherine, whom he taught to read and write (when he met her, she was illiterate), assisted him devoutly. In 1774 Blake opened with his wife, and younger brother, Robert, a print shop, but the venture failed after the death of Robert, in 1787. In 1784 he had begun working with the radical publisher Joseph Johnson. It was at Johnson's house that he met some of the leading intellectual dissidents of the time in England, including: Joseph Priestly, scientist; Richard Price, philosopher; John Henry Fuseli, painter; Mary Wollstonecraft, an early feminist; Thomas Paine, an American revolutionary, etc.

Around the year 1800 Blake moved to a cottage at Felpham, Sussex, to take up a job illustrating the work of William Hayley, a poet. It was in his cottage that Blake wrote *Milton, A Poem*, published later between 1805-1808. During 1790 and 1800 Blake was very active, composing most of his best known poems.

Blake returned to London in 1802 and began to write and illustrate *Jerusalem* (1804-1820). At the age of sixty-five he began to illustrate *The Book of Job*.

In the spring and summer of 1825 Blake had been taken severely ill. In late June he made a journey to Hampstead, after an apparent return of good health. Close to death Blake's mental occupation was in his art. He worked on the illustrations to Dante's *Inferno*. He died on August 12, 1827.

Just before passing, Blake began to sing hymns and verses. In a letter, George Richmond gives the following account: "He died [...] in a most glorious manner. He said He was going to that Country He had all his life wished to see, and expressed Himself Happy, hoping for Salvation through Jesus Christ—Just before he died His Countenance became fair. His eyes Brighten'd and he burst out Singing of the things he saw in Heaven."[5]

His funeral was a modest one. He was taken to Dissenter's burial ground in Bunhill Fields. Later on, on the day of Catherine's death, in October 1831, she also was calm and cheerful like her husband, and she called to him as if he were in the next room that she was coming to him, it would not be long.

This small account seems to describe the life of an average man, even if we asserted from the beginning that he was a great poet. Things are a little bit different.

Blake knew the wonders *within* man. He tried to *enlighten his fellow men* by revealing the powers they could attain from within themselves if they but put to use various, simple, natural laws.

In order to be able to understand Blake's poems, Blake's teachings (as we believe that, knowing more than an ordinary man, even possessing some sort of secret knowledge, he also would have liked his beliefs to come true), one should first become acquainted with some important aspects of Blake's personality. These would be: his *relief engraving* as a particular method of printing; his *visions*; his opinions concerning *Imagination*; his *religious belief*; his opinions as a *Rosicrucian* adept; his method in *poetry writing*. It also seems worth mentioning that all these aspects should be considered as acting simultaneously in Blake's art, often known as *composite art*.

In 1788, at the age of thirty-one, Blake began to experiment with relief etching. Blake's education involved the heavy work of preparing plates for etching and engraving, cutting, polishing, shaping plates, rubbing them with soot. Blake invented *relief etching* in order to be able to print and publish his own books. In traditional intaglio etching, the design must first be impressed in wax and then transferred to the plate with acid. Blake reversed the method. He painted the designs directly onto the plate with acid-resistant varnish, so as when it was treated with acid, the design remained in relief. This allowed Blake to write his poetry directly on the plates albeit *backwards* alongside his images, without the use of a printing press. The next step was to colour each book by hand and stitch them together. This method is known as *Illuminated Printing*.[6] Blake declared that coloring did not depend on where the colors are put, but on where the lights and dark are put, and all depends on form or outline, on where that is put; where that is wrong, the coloring never can be right.[7]

He said that he learned this new method in a dream, when his brother Robert, who was dead at that time, appeared and told him minutely what to do. However, Blake used the Illuminated Printing for some books, such as: *All Religions Are One*-prose work; *Songs of Innocence* (1789); *The Marriage of Heaven and Hell* (1790-1793)-prose work; *Visions of the Daughters of Albion* (1793); *The Book of Urizen* (1794); *Songs of Experience* (1794); *The Book of Los* (1795); *Milton: a Poem* (1804); *Jerusalem: The Emanation of the Giant Albion* (1804-1820).

Visions were a sustaining force for William Blake throughout his artistic and poetic life. At the age of four, he saw God "put his head to the window" and at nine, he saw "a tree full of angles." These visions increased in time, and the world of angels and dreams made its way into Blake's highly prolific artistic life—his poetry, engravings, and watercolors.[8] All these visions he had seemed but natural to him. He believed in them, but neither did they belong to an insane person, nor took place in another world. According to Blake, all this happened in this world, only man's power of seeing was insufficient to *percieve* them.

Blake told one of his intimate friends that he had the power of bringing his *imaginations* before his mind's eye so clearly that he could not go wrong in designing them. He also said that he was often the companion of spirits who taught and advised him. His painting of *The Vision of Jacob's Ladder* will reveal to most mystics to what Blake was referring. He likewise declared that he had the power of calling upon personages of ancient times, to talk with them of their painting methods. His own creations were compared, strangely enough, with those of the cinquecento period. He held the works of Raphael and Michael Angelo in deep veneration.[9] *Imagination* was the word Blake used when alluding to True Spiritual Life, the only real life in Blake's opinion. It was the very *archetype* of the human life, as Karl Gustav Young would say, and it also was the predominant Truth Blake expounded throughout his entire life. It may be summed up in some of his own lines:

> Nature has no Outline, but Imagination has. Nature has no Tune, but Imagination has. Nature has no Supernatural and dissolves; Imagination is Eternity.[10]

Blake, like all mystics, believed in a double-leveled existence: the Material Life (what we see around us) and the Spiritual Life, the only real one. According to him the Spiritual Life is Imagination (Eternity). Imagination helps us create everything we take as life (in fact only a faint shadow of it—Platonic viewpoint).

On the other hand, what he calls the Poetic Genius is the True Man that creates the material outline of man as we see him. Both the Spiritual Life (Imagination) and the Poetic Genius are *archetypes* of the material world, the only possibility to make man *eternal* as he should be.

In order to complete Blake's picture, his *religious belief* doubtlessly is a matter of major importance. Blake's family were Dissenters,[11] and seemed to have belonged to the Moravian sect.[12] The Bible had an early and also lasting effect upon Blake, and would remain a crucial source of inspiration throughout his life. Yet, he followed a religion of his own. He himself admits:

> I know of no other Christianity, and of no other Gospel than the liberty both of body and mind to exercise the Divine Arts of Imagination: Imagination, the real and eternal World of which this Vegetable Universe is but a faint shadow, and in which we shall live in our Eternal or Imaginative Bodies, when these Vegetable Mortal Bodies are no more.[13]

Kazin, one of Blake's biographers, says about him that he was a libertarian obsessed with God; a mystic who reversed the mystical pattern, for he sought man as the end of his search. He was a Christian who hated the churches; a revolutionary who abhorred the materialism of the radicals.[14] Blake was a non-conformist who hated being forced to believe what he did not. He abhorred slavery and believed in racial and sexual equality. Several of his poems and paintings express a notion of *universal humanity*. For him men were all alike, although various.[15] He rejected all forms of imposed authority and his views on what he saw as oppression and restriction of rightful freedom included the Church as well. Blake was a follower of Unitarian philosophy.[16] His spiritual beliefs are given in his volume *Songs of Innocence* (1794). Like the Gnostics, he distinguished between the Old Testament God, whom he rejected for being cruel, and the New Testament God (manifested through Jesus Christ), whom he saw as a positive influence, but not more than that. He believed in One non-manifested, eternal God who created the World. He portrayed the upper class institutions and the Church of England as corrupt and exploiters of the weak in society. Blake dreamed of an idyllic England, free from corruption, an idea that appears in the poem *The*

Echoing Green. He also was a pioneering *vegetarian*. A friend of his says about him:

> He was more like the ancient pattern of virtue than I ever expected to see in this world; he feared nothing so much as being rich, lest he should lose his spiritual riches. He was at the same time the most sublime in his expressions, with the simplicity and gentleness of a child.[17]

Blake liked children very much and even wondered how sincerely children enjoyed his poems. He believed in the genuine innocence children usually have. Believing in freedom and equality, he was among the writers who were pro-revolution and sustained the French Revolution, not knowing what would happen in the future. Blake saw the French Revolution as an Apocalypse, the beginning of a *new age*. As a matter of fact, Blake joined for a time the Swedenborgian Church of the New Jerusalem in London.[18]

As mentioned before, Blake did not believe in any religion. In fact he considered religious cults as being created by people and being related to power. Viscomi, another biographer of his, even stresses upon the fact that he was a deeply spiritual poet, yet very opposed to organized religion.[19] His opinions about religion are to be found in the first two illuminated books he created: *All Religions Are One* and *There is No Natural Religion*. The ideas expressed here are daring and strange at the same time:

- Man's perceptions are not bound by organs of perception; he *perceives more than sense* can discover (I).
- If any could desire what he is incapable of possessing, despair must be his eternal lot (VI).
- The *desire of man being infinite*, the possession is Infinite & himself Infinite (VII).

Consequently, he who sees the Infinite in all things sees God. He who sees the Ratio, only sees himself. Therefore, *God becomes as we are, that we may be as he is*.

The main principles Blake based his conceptions on are able to explain many of the words he used in his poems, as well as his attitude. These principles are as follows:

- Principle 1. That the Poetic Genius is the true Man, and that the body of outward form of Man is derived from the Poetic Genius. Likewise that the forms of all things are derived from their Genius, which by the Ancients was called an Angel & Spirit & Demon.

- Principle 2. As all men are alike in outward form, So (and with the same infinite variety) all are alike in the Poetic Genius.
- Principle 3. No man can think, write or speak from his heart, but he must intend truth, thus all sects of Philosophy are from the Poetic Genius adapted to the weakness of every individual.
- Principle 4. As none by travelling overknown lands can find out the unknown, So from already acquired knowlegde Man could not acquire more; therefore an universal Poetic Genius exists.
- Principle 5. The Religions of all Nations are derived from each Nation's different reception of the Poetic Genius, which is every where called the Spirit of Prophecy.
- Principle 6. The Jewish & Christian Testaments are An original derivation from the Poetic Genius. This is necessary from the confined nature of bodily sensation.
- Principle 7. As all men are alike (tho' infinitely various), So all Religions, &, as all similars, have one source. The true Man is the source, he being the Poetic Genius.[20]

One may say that it was his Poetic Genius that arose opposed ideas concerning the poet's mental health, but, again, things are a bit more complicated than they seem and different as well.

Although a very strong personality, Blake suffered for not being understood. The lack of public recognition sent him into a severe depression which lasted from 1810 to 1817, and even close friends thought him *insane*. The truth is that this very aspect occupies an important position in Blake's being accepted for what he was in society. Some of his contemporaries called him a harmless lunatic. Eaves[21] says about him:

> My personal opinion is that he suffered from a kind of schizophrenia. He saw visions, heard voices. Later in his life he claimed that he was not a poet, but that his poems were dictated to him.[22]

Linnell,[23] in his turn, said:

> I never saw anything the least like madness, for I never opposed him spitefully as many did but being really anxious to fathom if possible the amount of truth which might be in his most startling assertions I generally met with a sufficient rational explanation in the most really friendly and conciliatory tone.[24]

Nobody knows what the exact truth is, but those who did not find him insane are those who admired him for his *profound wisdom*.

Among all the famous *Rosicrucian* painters and poets in the late 18th century and early 19th century, Blake stands out as one of the most illuminated minds through whom Cosmic Wisdom flowed. In being able to symbolize great Truths, in art and writing, Blake is without a peer. His paintings and poems revealed to the men of his time what the occult philosophy of Jacob Boehme[25] had revealed to 16th century Europe.[26]

Compared with his contemporaries, Blake had a quite different approach to *nature*. With him nature is not the mere objective image of a thought or feeling, neither is it an image of the past, ruins, graveyards, etc. as it used to be with most of his contemporary poets.

Blake's attitude is due to a different perception of Nature. It appeared to him in the *Royal Splendor of her True Self.* Nature's True Self was its spiritual self, an inner, invisible self, perceived by some only. It was, again, a kind of *archetype*, different from what ordinary people call "nature." Hence Blake's being little understood by those around him; hence the idea that he was insane. But in order to get the True Self of Nature man was required *imagination* (also vision), since Nature was populated with angels, spirits and demons.[27]

As a Rosicrucian adept, Blake was revealed the Divine Wonders of the Universe and the secrets of Nature. But the only capable one to perceive this beautiful world was the *man of Imagination*. He himself explained what the nature looked like in this man's eyes: *Nature is Imagination itself.* It is Man that creates nature, *since as a man is, so he sees*. This very statement explains the essence of such a viewpoint: Life is nothing else but what man wants or is able to see.

I am not ashamed, afraid, or averse to tell you what ought to be told; that I am under the direction of messengers from heaven, daily and nightly.[28]

Blake lived like many Rosicrucian mystics with utter indifference to all worldly wealth. And, after all what has been said here about him, one may wonder what kind of person Blake actually was. Very many contemporaries, as well as many other later critics, painters and poets, tried to explain Blake's Truths. It might be interesting and also worth trying to summarize some of Blake's opinions, and those of some people who knew him well enough in order to draw Blake's psychological outline. We start from the idea that William Blake was a great mysterious personality of his time (and not only), but also an Initiate (possessing some occult knowledge) and, therefore, one may learn from him, besides what he says in and through his artistic work, some important life lessons. Here are some ideas related to this aspect:

- Blake had the *Bible* as an important and early source of inspiration.
- According to him there is *no natural religion*. All religions are based on authority, and, consequently, he was against them, as he was against churches and priests.
- He believed in *equality* among all people: racial and sexual equality, the *liberty* of body and mind and rejected any form of authority. He believed in the existence of *two Gods* (Gnosticism): an evil one, who created this unfair world, and a positive one, invisible, having the supreme power and who created the Universe. It is the latter that people should strive to reach. His belief in a "universal humanity" proves his love for human beings; hence, his wish to help people by teaching them what he knew and they could not see yet.
- He was a pioneering *vegetarian*.
- Visconti says about him that he *wanted to be an artist* and he knew it, but he had to settle for craftsman status first. The choice was important. It taught him that you *can't separate invention from execution*.
- *Visions* supported his whole work.
- Life is more than what a man gets through his senses. It goes beyond senses; it is *imagination*: "If the doors of perception were cleansed everything would appear to man as it is—infinite [...]. For man has closed himself up till he sees all things through narrow chinks of his cavern."[29]
- Alfred Kazin mentions the fact that Blake *never* traveled. Except for one three-year stay at a cottage in Sussex, he hardly went out of London.[30] He might have chosen this attitude knowing that there is no other possibility of undertaking a *spiritual journey* instead of travelling in the material world.
- Blake used to say that all those who aspire must go, at least once, through a period of despair. This statement reminds us of the pains and despair a candidate felt while passing through a ritual of initiation.

- He was not a rich man, yet he was known to be *very charitable*.
- He kept telling about the spiritual entities he was surrounded by, and continued: "I shall leave any one in this country astonished at my *patience* and *forbearance* of injuries upon injuries. I was commanded by my spiritual friends to bear all and be silent, and go through all without murmuring. It is said that after having been through the ordeal of Initiation the candidate is resurrected; from that moment on he is a completely different person. A better, more understanding one.
- But it is T.S. Eliot who managed to draw a conclusion regarding Blake's personality, and this conclusion might also offer an answer to many other people who wonder why they are rejected by the society they live in, and, paradoxically, although harmless, people seem to be afraid of them. T.S. Eliot says about Blake that he approached everything with a mind unclouded by current opinions. "There was nothing of the superior person about him. *That makes him terrifying*."[31]

It is obvious that Blake taught people by means of all he did as an artist, as a poet and as a man some lessons worth taking into account. But a question arises here: did he teach how ordinary men may become Men of Imagination? (as he spoke mostly about himself and his convictions). The answer is "yes." Behind his lines there also are some ways, some requirements which might help anybody to reach a higher spiritual level:

- The person should like to engage himself/herself in such an endeavour.
- To be and remain open to all that comes towards him/her, and be able to decide what is genuine from what is not.
- To be ready to work hard, as reaching God is far more difficult than we usually think it is. Subsequently, such a person will get trained how to progress in work, how to perceive the Infinite.
- To be able to understand that the *only* path to the unique God is Love.

We think it is necessary and positive as well to take at least some of his pieces of advice.

NOTES

1. Emmanuel von Swedenborg (1688-1772) is a Swedish philosopher, theologian, chemist, anatomist, and mystic, fluent in eleven languages.

Swedenborg devoted the first half of his life to scientific investigations. Thereafter he turned his full attention to theology, metaphysics and started to explore mystical experience. Among Swedenborg's most popular books are Heaven and Hell and Earths in Universe. His spiritual writing influenced Emerson, Goethe, Henry James Sr., Dostoevsky, and William Blake. During his life, Swedenborg published over 50 works. His books have been translated into some thirty languages.

"There are two worlds, a spiritual world where angels and spirits are, and a natural world where men are" (from True Christian Religion). After a close-to-death experience, Swedenborg was convinced that he had been designated by God as a spiritual emissary to explore higher planets and to report the findings to humankind. He entered ecstatic trances, visiting heaven and hell.

2. The William Blake Page, Web Museum, David Ross and Britain Express; also see: http:// en.wikipedia.org/wiki/William_Blake.
3. http://www. newi.ac.uk/rdover/blake/Life.htm.
4. Wikipedia, 3.
5. Grison, *Samuel Palmer*, 38; here in Wikipedia, *ed.cit.*, 6.
6. "Illuminated" refers to the use of bright colours in the way they were used in medieval paintings.
7. William H. McKegg, F.R.C., *William Blake—Painter, Poet and Mystic*, in "The Rosicrucian Digest," May 1932; here in http:// www. geocities.com/ Athens/Acropolis/2216, 1.
8. *The Visions of William Blake.*
9. William H. McKegg, F.R.C., *op.cit.*, 2.
10. *Idem*, 5.
11. Religious Dissidents; they opposed the principles of the Anglican Church.
12. Wikipedia, 2.
13. William McKegg, F.R.C., *op.cit.*, 4.
14. Rachel Galvin, *William Blake: Visions and Verses*, here in: http:// www. neh.gov/news/humanities/2004-05/blake.html+William+Blake+visions &hl=ro&gl=ro&ct=clnk&cd=2.
15. Wikipedia, 4.
16. The Unitarian Church was founded by Socinus Faustus (1539-1604) an Italian theologian. The Unitarians do not recognise the Trinity as well as the divinity of Jesus Christ. According to them the Holy Spirit is not a special person, and Jesus Christ is not mankind's Redeemer, the Mysteries are useful, but not absolutely neccesary. They also deny the existence of the Original Sin. It is interesting to mention that Socinus Faustus traveled to Transylvania in 1574.

17. In Linda S. Santucci, *William Blake*, 2000-2003.
18. http:// William_Blake.org.
19. Rachel Galvin, *loc.cit.*
20. Hypertext pages based on a Helpfile created by Richard Dover in: http://www.newi.ac.uk/rdover/blake/allrels1.htm.
21. Eaves is a professor at the University of Rochester. He is working with Robert Essik of the University of California, Riverside, and Joseph Viscomi of the University of North Carolina, Chapel Hill, to change the way Blake is understood. Since 1996 the three have struggled to create the Blake Archive, a website meant to accomplish the knowledge and necessary information about Blake.
22. Rachel Galvin, *op.cit.*, 2.
23. John Linnell was a young artist whom Blake met when he returned to London, in 1802. It was through Linnell that he met Samuel Palmer, who belonged to a group of artists who called themselves the Shoreham Ancients. His members rejected modern trends and believed in a spiritual New Age as Blake himself did. Linnell also helped him to receive the commission for Dante's *Inferno.*
24. Rachel Galvin, *op.cit.*, 5.
25. Jacob Boehme (Jakob Behmen) (1575-1624) is a German mystic and early modern philosopher. He is known for his radical vision of God as including a negative, painful aspect. He influenced the English Anabaptists, and later on had a strong influence upon the German Romantics. He wrote: *Society: Philosophy: History of Philosophy: Early Modern* and *Society: Religion and Spirituality: Esoteric and Occult.*
26. William H. McKegg, *op.cit.*, 1.
27. *Idem.*
28. *Idem*, 3.
29. William Blake; here in William H. McKegg, 4.
30. Alfred Kazin's biographical book about Blake was entitled: *The Inmost Leaf.*
31. Rachel Galvin, *loc.cit.*

The Return of the Native in the Light of the Carnivalesque

AJOY SENGUPTA

O for a draught of vintage! that hath been
    Cool'd a long age in the deep-delvéd earth,
Tasting of Flora and the country green,
    Dance, and Provençal song, and sunburnt mirth!

John Keats

AFTER writing five novels in five years Hardy possibly felt the necessity of a short break in order to brood over the line of his future action. After completing *The Hand of Ethelberta*, Hardy informed his publisher: 'I do not wish to attempt any more original writing of any length for a few months, until I can learn the best line to take for the future' (Turner 57). In May, 1876 Hardy and Emma set out for a continental tour. They returned to England in June and after a few days, on 3 July 1876, they settled in a 'pretty cottage overlooking the Dorset Stour—called Riverside Villa [...] at Sturminster Newton [...]. It was their first house and, though small, probably that in which they spent their happiest days' (Millgate 114-15). Turner claims, they wished to produce there two things, a book and a baby. 'The book did materialize, but not immediately [...]. Back in Dorset, he started planning a novel about the return of a native, set in the immediate neighbourhood of his birthplace' (Turner 58). After the Christmas that year the couple returned to Sturminster and with an overwhelming image of the vast heath behind the Bockhampton cottage inscribed on his imagination, Hardy began to jot down about 'the vast tract of unenclosed wild known as Egdon Heath' (*RN* 2). The novel was serially published in *Belgravia* throughout 1878.

Millgate observes, 'Much of the remembered happiness of the Sturminster Newton period had its source in the generous and confident flow of Hardy's creative energies as he worked on the manuscript of *The Return of the Native*' (197). The delightful description of the jovial rustics around the bonfire or at wedding fiesta or at Christmas rejoicings must have been inspired by that happiness.

In 1879 the Rabelais Club was founded by Walter Besant who, inviting Hardy to join the club, had praised *The Return of the Native* as 'the most original the most virile and most humorous of all modern novels' (Millgate 208). Hardy attended the Club thrice, the first visit being in 1879.

The entire action of *The Return of the Native* is enacted within the periphery of the Egdon Heath that 'had an ancient permanence which the sea cannot claim' (*RN* 5). In this vast stretch of ancient space Hardy situates the novel, and weaves it around ancient folk festivals of pagan origin. In the essay "Hardy and Folklore" [in *A Norton Critical Edition* of *The Return of the Native*] James Gindin points out:

> [...] the principal action of the novel takes a year, from one Guy Fawkes night to the next; the long scene in which Eustacia Vye and Clym Yeobright become acquainted with each other takes place at an ancient mummers' play performed every Christmas; the final section of the novel, the extension of the time scheme required to bring Diggory Venn and Thomasin together, is centered on the communal dance around the maypole. (396)

Gindin also observes that the folk ceremonies which are portrayed by Hardy and which continued to exist in Dorset and other South Western countries in the nineteenth century, contained both residual pagan and Christian elements. The bonfires of Guy Fawkes' night on 5 November each year not only commemorated the saving of the state from Roman Catholic plotters in 1605, but also the pagan ceremony which utilized the fire to tame the power of the ensuing winter and to commemorate the dead of the past year. For the local community of the heath 'the bonfire is public, ceremonial and connected with a set of established traditions' (396).

The ceremony, which manifests purely pagan folk culture, is the dance of the rustics around the maypole, a pre-Christian celebration of fertility in summer, which ultimately unites Venn and Thomasin. These two characters along with some other jovial and happy rustics are 'lighter, free to live following the ancient world of the seasons without being tortured by guilt, excessive ambition, or the wish to be other than they are' (Gindin 397).

The vital force of the rustic community, their enduring vigour, their zest for festive occasions make them emerge triumphant over the gloom of their surrounding atmosphere. The tragic atmosphere that affects the psyche of the protagonists fails to suppress the rustics' flair for rejoicing.

The stern environment of the heath, which forces them to accept cutting thorny furze as their profession, cannot reduce their positive attitude towards mirth and merriment. On the contrary,

> The heath does nourish this community; more, it nourishes the vitality, the purposeful staying power, *the continuing mirth*, which sustain and are sustained by the community's labour. (Brown 56) [emphasis added]

The primitive rurals are not daunted by their tough professions or hard schedules. Despite their everyday struggle their vitality establishes itself more vigorously than that of the modern urbans. In the essay, "Hardy's Major Fiction," John Holloway observes, 'throughout the book the stress falls on the revitalizing power of rural life, and on how its vitality is intrinsically greater than that of modernity' (Guerard 53). Clym, who having been fed up with the false glamour of Paris returned to his native place Egdon, was revitalized by the flora and fauna of the heath and its surroundings. Those who rebelled against the antiquity and age-old traditional way of life ultimately perished in the battle of existence. Persons yearning for the urban ways, like Eustacia, cannot survive while the rustics can. Holloway observes:

> The whole rural ambience can ultimately assert a greater vitality than the city life from which Clym has come. As he gives himself to it, he is regenerated from a basic source. By the end, Egdon has triumphed, even if on its own stern terms. The novel resolves in an assertion of the old order, its regenerative austerity, its rewarding unrewardingness. (Guerard 54)

The rustics who are firmly rooted in Egdon and the old order it represents, are to provide the elements of mirth which off set the grimness of the story. The rural characters such as Grandfer Cantle, his son Christian Cantle, Timothy Fairway, Susan Nunsuch, Olly Dowden, Humphrey, Sam, *et al.*, are instrumental in introducing the reader to the local celebrations, rituals, beliefs, superstitions and professions. That life is not all struggle, is exhibited by their buoyant joviality whenever festive occasions offer a congenial situation. Douglas Brown observes,

> The deeply-rooted communal life expresses itself in the bonfire ritual and the wedding rejoicings, in the mumming, and the fair, and the effigy [...]. The deep source of this life of the heath hamlets is in dark and fecund Egdon itself; and it will persist, through whatever catastrophe, numbed, but strong. (63)

After the famous opening chapter introducing the reader to the Egdon Heath and the following chapter where 'Humanity Appears upon the Scene Hand in Hand with Trouble' (*RN* 5), we meet the offsprings of the soil—the rustic bystanders—in the third chapter titled 'The Custom of the Country.' The rustics pile up furge faggots in the form of a pyramid of thirty feet circumference at the top of Rainbarrow. While they have been building the heap, thirty bonfires like 'red suns and tufts of fire one by one began to arise, flecking the whole country round' (*RN* 11). In this context the author openly evokes and invokes the Bacchanal spirit. Some of the fires are like 'Maenades,' the Greek worshippers of Bacchus, the wine-god. The jubilant crowd lights the bonfire to commemorate the Gunpowder plot (Guy Fawkes' Day), but probably the fire is also connected with the rituals of Druids, the pre-Christian priests, and Saxon ceremonies. The heath becomes luminous with the bonfire—

> The first tall flame from Rainbarrow sprang into the sky, [...]. The cheerful blaze streaked the inner surface of the human circle—now increased by other stragglers, male and female—with its own gold livery, and even overlaid the dark turf around with a lively luminousness [...]. It seemed as if the bonfire-makers were standing in some radiant upper storey of the world, detached from and independent of the dark stretches below. (*RN* 11)

The bonfire enlightens the inherent vitality of the rustics. Their power of enjoying the revelry is kindled by its flames. For the moment, being oblivious of the scuffles of life, they feel themselves exalted to an elevated level of merriment. Adjourning all the cares of life, they relish the occasion blithely.

The ancient ritual of the rural community functions as a 'spontaneous resistance to the dark fiat of nature' (Brown 57).

> To light a fire is the instinctive and resistant act of man when, at the winter ingress, the curfew is sounded throughout Nature. (*RN* 12)

The bleak surface of the heath and its impending gloom are challenged by the vivacity of its inhabitants. The heath seems to foster this virility and stability of these rustics. Douglas Brown observes,

> The brooding darkness of the heath lit by the labourers' bonfires, repeats the crashing storm defied by Oak's persistence. The heath, it appears, nourishes the very vitality and stability it would threaten to destroy; and the vitality and the stability together penetrate the interchange of voices from which the tale itself now emerges. (57)

Hardy's rustics emerge gradually and tantalizingly from the darkness of the night. The bright light and dark shades on the body and the garments of the congregation manifest them as a work of Dürer (1471-1528), the famous German painter and engraver:

> The brilliant lights and sooty shades which struggled upon the skin and clothes of the persons standing round caused their lineaments and general contours to be drawn with Düreresque vigour and dash. (*RN* 12)

Incidentally, Dürer's picture celebrates the bucolic mirth at a carnival gathering. As J.B. Bullen in *The Expressive Eye* maintains, "Dürer's own *Dancing Peasants* was described in similar terms by William Bell Scott [in *Albert Dürer: His Life and Works* 214] in an 1869 edition of the engravings. It is, he says, 'a group full of vigour and enjoyment, the sturdy little woman being as strong and frisky as a young bear.' In *Under the Greenwood Tree* Hardy had already exploited the vigour of the scene, but the spirited 'dash' of Dürer's engraving stands in strong contrast to the quieter pictures of English and Dutch life which had inspired the scenes of the earlier novel. In *Under the Greenwood Tree* the distortion introduced into the descriptions of the Mellstock choir is simply comic in its effect (98-99). Here the merry group attains a sudden and amazing metamorphosis around the carnival fire.

> Shadowy eye-sockets, deep as those of a death's head, suddenly turned into pits of lustre: a lantern jaw was cavernous, then it was shining; wrinkles were emphasized to ravines, or obliterated entirely by a changed ray. Nostrils were dark wells; sinews in old necks were gilt mouldings; things with no particular polish on them were glazed; bright objects, such as the tip of a furze-hook one of the men carried, were as glass; eyeballs glowed like little lanterns. Those whom Nature had depicted as merely quaint became grotesque, the grotesque became preternatural; for all was in extremity. (*RN* 18)

It is this emphasis on the 'grotesque' in Hardy's depiction of the rustic joviality that would inevitably remind a reader of our times of Bakhtin's approach to the carnivalesque. The 'grotesque' has also been privileged over the classical in Bakhtin's study of Rabelais, indeed so much so, as to provoke the reviewers' comment, 'outside the grotesque there is no salvation' (Emerson 98). As Emerson rightly perceives, "the specific locus" of the "carnival space" is "the vulnerable, yet superbly shame-free, grotesque body" (163).

The festive atmosphere lends an added shine to the rural ambience and the inherent exuberance transforms the common rustics into extraordinary creatures. The luminous glow of the fire turns their common or even distorted features illuminated and jubilant. The light of the bonfire confronts the dark drabness of the heath. As Harold Bloom observes,

> *The Return of the Native* is concerned with the Promethean struggle of conscious life against the unconscious "rayless" universe from which it sprang. The poetic-dramatic structure of the first chapters initiates the underlying metaphor of the novel, the ancient conflict of light and darkness. The white man-made road that crosses the brown heath, the red glow of bonfires, the "blood-coloured" figure of Diggory Venn, challenge the dark drabness of the earth. (57)

Around the bonfire the rustics evince an attitude which bears direct correspondence with the Rabelaisian spirit of carnival. Grandfer Cantle, the most veteran and most jovial member of the congregation, is elated by the glimmering 'conflagration':

> The beaming sight, and the penetrating warmth, seemed to breed in him a cumulative cheerfulness, which soon amounted to delight. (*RN* 13)

He begins to dance by himself singing a song in which the king wishes to go to the queen along with the earl marshal to hear a penitential confession from her—

'The king′ call'd down′ his no-bles all′,
    by one′, by two′, by three′;
Earl Mar′-shal, I'll′ go shrive′ the queen′,
    And thou′ shalt wend′ with me′.
'A boon′, a boon′, quoth Earl′ Mar-shal′,
    And fell′ on his bend′-ded knee′,
That what′-so-e'er′ the queen′ shall say′,
    No harm′ there-of ′ may be′.' (*RN* 13)

This portion of the traditional Dorset ballad called *Earl Marshal* (also known as *The Jovial Crew* or *Queen Eleanor's Confession*), which still exists there, obviously 'uncrowns' the queen who is going to confess her fault. This uncrowning manifests a carnival spirit. The rural bystanders frequently take chance of festive occasions to subvert the grandeur or authority of the high and mighty. Grandfer feels that he becomes younger while dancing and singing around the fire. He takes a pause for a while to enquire whether they should go that night to the Quiet Woman Inn to congratulate Thomasin and Wildeve who are thought to have already been united in the bond of matrimony (actually the wedding had not taken place; Thomasin and Wildeve had gone to the Anglebury church while the marriage license had been made out for the Budmouth as the latter had not bothered to read the license). When Fairway replies in negative, the jovial old man protests and insists that they must go, and continues the ballad song—

> "Do thou′ put on′ a fri′-ar's coat′,
> And I'll′ put on′ a-no′-ther,
> And we′ will to′ Queen Ele′anor go′,
> Like Fri′ar and′ his bro′ther." (*RN* 14)

Here by 'queen' Grandfer must have meant Thomasin, but when in the ballad the king proposes that he and the earl marshal should go to hear the confession of Queen Eleanor in the disguise of friars, this also in a way shows the daring to mock both the royal persona and the church official. Besides, in this context Grandfer Cantle means to identify himself and his fellow rustic with friars, which is an oblique way of overthrowing the social hierarchy—a characteristic feature of the carnival attitude.

The rustics function as rich source of information about the major characters and action of the novel. From their conversation, it is revealed that Mrs. Yeobright initially had not given her consent to the wedding. Fairway informs that during the forbidding he had been present at the church 'which was a very curious thing to happen' (*RN* 15). This comment and their subsequent conversation expose their casual attitude towards the church and reveal their disregard for the ecclesiastical authority:

> 'I ha'n't been there to-year; and now the winter is a-coming on I won't say I shall.' [said the Grandfer]
> 'I ha'n't been these three years,' said Humphrey; 'for I'm so dead sleepy of a Sunday; and 'tis so terrible far to get there; and when you do get there 'tis such a mortal poor chance that you'll be chose for up above, when so many bain't, that I bide at home and don't go at all.' (*RN* 15)[1]

During the conversation when Fairway observes that they cannot blame Wildeve and Thomasin who has not invited anyone at their wedding, as dancing on such occasions often affects the legs of men particularly of the age above forty, Grandfer objects vehemently and asserts—

> You be bound to dance at Christmas because 'tis the time o' year; you must dance at weddings because 'tis the time o' life. (*RN* 17)

Their zest for merry-making is further manifested more vigorously in the next part of his comment—

> '[...] For my part I like a good hearty funeral as well as anything. You've as splendid victuals and drink as at other parties, and even better.' (*RN* 17)

This remark also brings out their denial to be overwhelmed by the apprehension of demise which is an inevitable termination of life. To defy death is a carnival disposition, and the rustics refuse to let go any chance of eating and consuming liquor as on such occasions normal strenuous life is suspended for the time being.

The character of Christian Cantle, though somewhat pathetic, is humorously built. He is 'the man no woman will marry' (*RN* 19) as confessed by himself. He comes to this inference after proposing and being rejected by several women. The last woman he proposed, replied (as reported by Christian himself) 'Get out of my sight, you slack-twisted, slim-looking maphrotite fool' (*RN* 19).

The interpretation given by Christian's mother of the cause of such ill luck again reflects delightful earthy humor. When he was born, there was no moon and his mother said 'No moon, no man' (*RN* 20). This concurrence was drawn from a traditional superstition that virility was connected with the full moon while on the contrary 'no moon' would naturally suggest lack of vigour and luck. At the same time this uninhibited preoccupation with the body, sex, lower bodily stratum brings out a latent carnival spirit which still existed among these lowly people whereas it had already disappeared from the upper strata of society. Thus Christian and Fairway carry on their conjectures about the size of the moon at one's birth and its proportionate impact on the (future) virility of the new-born concerned. Christian asks him whether the moon was 'terrible full' (*RN* 20) when Fairway was born. The former replies, 'Well, 'a was not new' (*RN* 20).

Similarly funny is Christian's apprehension of ghosts. Based on the report of a little boy, Johny Nunsuch (Susan's son), who had mistaken the reddleman to be a ghost, Timothy informs that an apparition has been seen of late in Egdon. Timothy's comment and Christian's reaction continue in the same vein.

> 'You'll have to lie alone all your life; and 'tis not to married couples but to single sleepers that a ghost shows himself when 'a do come. One has been seen lately, too. A very strange one.' (*RN* 20)

The proposal of congratulating the newly married couple and the rustics' subsequent remarks bring out once again their flair for merriment. Fairway said, '[…] I am no drinker, as we know, but when the womenfolk and youngsters have gone home we can drop down across to the Quiet Woman, and strike up a ballet in front of the married folk's door' (*RN* 21). The jovial Grandfer immediately agrees and says 'I'm as dry as a keg with biding up here in the wind, and I haven't seen the colour of drink since mammet-time today. 'Tis said that the last brew at the Woman is very pretty drinking' (*RN* 21). The old guy also promises that he will sing the 'Jovial Crew' or any other song on that occasion.

The rustics' attitude here also manifests their feature of fellow feeling. They are ever ready to witness any merry event of the county to display their support to and appreciation for such occasions. Unlike the aristocrat urbans, they are inclined to take share in the collective life and thereby participate jovially on every possible social occasion. Though Thomasin and Wildeve have not invited them, they humbly agree to perform their duty of wishing them happy conjugal life.

Though the bonfire gradually starts to die down, the jolly mood of the rustics hardly display any sign of decline. Fairway proposes Susan to have a jig with him and the next the congregation witnesses

> a vision of the matron's broad form whisking off towards the space whereon the fire had been kindled. She was lifted bodily by Mr. Fairway's arm, which had been flung round her waist before she had become aware of his intention. (*RN* 23)

Fairway's enthusiasm permeates through the gathering. The turf-cutter chooses Olly Dowden as his partner and dances with her likewise. The youths there, immediately inspired by the performance of their elders, select their individual maids and start dancing. Grandfer cantle jigs like a three-legged creature with his stick. Within a few seconds Rainbarrow witnesses the revolving of dark figures around the almost subsided bonfire—

> The chief noises were women's shrill cries, men's laughter, Susan's stays and pattens, Olly Dowden's 'heu-heu-heu!' and the strumming of the wind upon the furze-bushes, which formed a kind of a tune to the demoniac measure they trod. (*RN* 24)

Thus the merriment reaches its climax and becomes wild with the Saturnalian exuberance. The rural people's extraordinary ability to snatch enjoyment from the cup of drink becomes manifest. They resemble the tipsy team of the Lord of Misrule to form the laughing chorus. Here we have a manifestation or the true carnival spirit with its emphasis on bodily abandon: "as Bakhtin describes it in his *Rabelais*, the common language of bodies is of a certain highly convenient sort. [...] the body (and even more, the grotesque body) cannot make a misstep or mistake. It is already out of step [...]. This body is inviting and available to all without discrimination. [...] the grotesque body [...] is guaranteed triumph over classical form, institutional oppression, and individual death" (Emerson 163-64).

Chapter V of Book I, titled 'Perplexity among Honest People' depicts some of the rustics gathered in front of The Quiet Woman Inn who have congregated to compliment Wildeve and Thomasin on their supposed wedding. They turn up singing with bass viol and flute led by the Grandfer and Fairway. The couple along with Mrs. Yeobright is somewhat embarrassed by their presence as the marriage has not actually taken place for some misinterpretation already mentioned. However, Wildeve does not want to dampen the spirit of the congregation and instead of informing them about the mistake he accepts their compliment and treats them by offering a stone jar containing mead which instantly animates the rustics—

> 'That's a drop of the right sort, I can see,' said Grandfer cantle, with the air of a man too well-mannered to show any hurry to taste it.
> 'Yes,' said Wildeve, ' 'tis some old mead. I hope you will like it.'
> 'O ay!' replied the guests, in the hearty tones natural when the words demanded by politeness coincide with those of deepest feeling. 'There isn't, prettier drink under the sun.'
> 'I'll take my oath there isn't,' added Grandfer Cantle. 'All that can be said against mead is that 'tis rather heady, and apt to lie about a man a good while. But tomorrow's Sunday, thank God.' (*RN* 37)

When Wildeve asks whether they would like to drink in cups and glasses they express their eagerness to consume from a single beaker by passing it round. Thus their feeling of communal unity is expressed along with their inclination for Dionysian mirth.

Timothy observes that the woman whom Wildeve has got is as precious as a 'dimant' (*RN* 37) and her father was an expert player of clarionet and bass viol. Then follows a humorous description of Mr Yeobright's performance one Sunday at the Kingsbere church:

> One Sunday I can well mind—a bass viol day that time, and Yeobright had brought his own. 'Twas the Hundred-and-thirty-third to 'Lydia'; and when they'd come to 'ran down his beard and o'er his robes its costly moisture shed,' neighbour Yeobright, who had just warmed to his work, drove his bow into them strings that glorious grand that he e'en a'most sawed the bass-viol into two pieces. Every winder in church rattled as if 'twere a thunderstorm. Old Pa'son William lifted his hands in his great holy surplice as natural as if he'd been in common clothes, and seemed to say to hisself, 'O for such a man in our parish!' [...]. (*RN* 38-39)

This vigorous account of Yeobright's performance reveals the rustics' power of appreciating boisterous music and reminds one of the performance of Hardy's grandfather at the Stinsford church. Rutland observes, 'The comical description, in the fifth chapter, of the playing of the clarinet by Thomasin's father is a humorous reproduction of the tales which Hardy had heard in his youth of the prowess of his grandfather, Thomas Hardy the First' (182).

At the time of parting Grandfer offers to sing another song as he considers himself to be 'as full of notes as a bird' (*RN* 40). But Wildeve stops him politely saying that he would not trouble Grandfer at that moment, he would rather listen to his song some other day. The simple-hearted old man promises that he would learn ten new songs to entertain Wildeve at his next performance.

Chapter V of Book II, titled 'Through the Moonlight' portrays the collective mirth on the Christmas Eve at the residence of Mrs. Yeobright who has invited 'the plain neighbours and workpeople without drawing any lines, just to give 'em a good supper and such like' (*RN* 105). The supper is preceded by boisterous dance and revelry and the performance of the well-known mummer's play *Saint George* where the Turkish Knight's role is enacted by Eustacia in disguise. Other members of the mumming group are rustics like Humphrey, Sam, Fairway etc. Though 'they were not enthusiastic' about performing in mumming and they are used to participate in such 'a traditional pastime' (*RN* 96) only to carry on a tradition, yet the jovial dance preceding it is enjoyed by the rustics to their heart's content.

When the group of mummers approaches at close quarters of Mrs. Yeobright's dwelling they can comprehend that lively music and dance are progressing within. From the note of the serpent the mummers identifies it to be 'Nancy's Fancy' which is a well-known folk tune of the locality. The dance is proceeding at a place adjacent to the door: 'The brushing of skirts and elbows, sometimes the bumping of shoulders, could be heard against the very panels' (*RN* 104). The mumming team wait outside for the termination of the performance within so that they may secure the entrance. The musical instruments come to a pause, but the dancers continue with renewed vigour and enthusiasm:

> The air was now that one without any particular beginning, middle, or end, which perhaps, among all the dances which throng an inspired fiddler's fancy, best conveys the idea of the interminable—the celebrated 'Devil's Dream.' The fury of personal movement that was kindled by the fury of the notes could be approximately imagined by these outsiders under the moon, from the occasional kicks of toes and heels against the door, whenever the whirl round had been of more than customary velocity. (*RN* 105)

The 'Devil's Dream' which is also called 'The Devil Among the Tailors' is a famous six-handed reel, continues for a considerable time and 'the bumping against the door, the laughter, the stamping' (*RN* 105) are quite boisterous. The carnival atmosphere reigns supreme and when carnival festivity goes on, all other normal activities must remain suspended for the time being. The revellers at Mrs. Yeobright's house celebrate the Christmas eve amid extreme jubilation and mirth. Grandfer Cantle along with other rustics participates in this occasion displaying once again their capacity of rejoicing, laughing out the ordeals of life. The music and dancing are terminated with a vivacious agility—

> At this moment the fiddles finished off with a screech, amid the serpent emitted a last note that nearly lifted the roof. (*RN* 106)

The dance being over, the mummers are warmly greeted by the guests who earnestly want to sustain the festive fervour. The humpbacked father Christmas appears with a huge club, makes his inaugural speech concluding with—

> 'Make room, make room, my gallant boys,
>   And give us space to rhyme;
> We've come to show Saint George's play,
>   Upon this Christmas time.' (*RN* 106)

The Valiant Soldier, the Turkish Knight, Saint George, the Doctor and the Saracen make their entrance one by one and their parts are enacted by the performers satisfactorily.

Following the completion of the mummer's show the guests as well as the mummers are served supper, the menu including beef, bread, cake, pastry, mead and old wine (*RN* 112). Clym and his mother serve the supper so that their maidservant may have her food as a guest. Thus on this festive occasion the proletariats are entertained by their social superiors. This detail is reminiscent of the Roman Saturnalia of the Golden Age when masters used to serve the slaves, celebrating the reign of Saturn during the days of the carnival. Though here the mutual relation is not of master and slave, but the rustic invitees and the maidservant obviously belong to lower stratum of social hierarchy than Mrs. Yeobright and her son. Carnival features such as mass indulgence in riotous dance and music, consumption of victuals and liquor and inversion of social hierarchy are prominently focused in this celebration.

The play of *St. George* which had been seen several times by Hardy in his boyhood, was in vogue in Dorset for many generations. In 1920s he reconstructed the play from his memory and printed it privately in 1921. Twenty years before its reconstruction, he discussed about the play with William Archer, as described in *Real Conversations* (Rutland 180). Rutland observes, 'Beside the Heath, transmuted by Hardy's imagination into a Presence, there are also many smaller matters introduced into the novel which are faithfully painted from the real. The most obvious of these are the Christmas festivities at Mrs. Yeobright's house, which bear a close relationship to those described in *Under the Greenwood Tree*. But while the music of the choir was the centre of the early picture, that of the later is the play of St. George, which Hardy as a boy had seen acted many times' (Rutland 180).

The first chapter of Book VI titled 'The Inevitable Movement Onward' delineates the preparation and celebration of the Maypole in Egdon. Originally, the Maypole is an ancient emblem of fertility belonging to the beginning of Summer (Hole 136) and it is celebrated on the May Day. Christina Hole informs in her *British Folk Customs*,

> In the darkness of the early morning, the young people went out on May Day and cut down a tall, young tree, lopped off most of its branches, leaving only a few at the top, and so brought it home, to be adorned with flowers and garlands, and to serve as a centre for their dances. (136-37)

Here, in Egdon, all the youths from the adjacent area of a radius of two miles congregate in an open area beside Fairway's residence on the eve of Maypole. The pole is kept slanted with one terminal rested on a trestle and women are busy encircling the pole with garlands of fragrant wild flowers from the top downwards. The summit is wreathed with 'crossed hoops' (*RN* 298) of small flowers, beneath these follow one by one the zones of milk white May bloom, bluebells, cowslips, lilacs, ragged-robins, daffodils and other flowers garlanded up to the lowest part. Hardy portrays the jubilant preparation in a picturesque way. He observes—

> The *instincts of merry England* lingered on here with exceptional vitality, and the symbolic customs which tradition has attached to each season of the year were yet a reality on Egdon. Indeed, the impulses of all such outlandish hamlets are pagan still—in these spots homage to nature, self-adoration, frantic gaieties, fragments of Teutonic rites to divinities whose names are forgotten, seem in some way or other to have survived mediaeval doctrine. (*RN* 298) [emphasis added]

The next morning the Maypole can be seen erected at the centre of the green field, its summit penetrating into the sky. It is raised and set upright in the previous night or early morning by the young enthusiasts. Opening her casement and withdrawing the curtains Thomasin can see the pole. The fragrance of the charming sweet perfumed wild flowers has spread into the air of the surrounding arena and she is delighted to perceive the scent. Later, Hardy writes in *The Night of The Dance*:

> Yes; far and night things seem to know
> Sweet scenes are impending here;
> That all is prepared; that the hour is near
> For welcomes, fellowships, and flow
> Of sally, song, and cheer;
>
> That spigots are pulled and viols strung;
> That soon will arise the sound
> Of measures trod to tunes renowned;
>
> (ll 11-18) [Norton Critical Edition 396]

In the afternoon people start to congregate on the field. Clym observes the proceedings interestedly from an open window of his room. He sees Thomasin dressed gaily and appreciates her prettiness. The zealous brass band arrives about five o' clock and strikes up 'with apparently wind enough among its members to blow down his house' (*RN* 299). The boisterous dancing and music continue almost for four hours. Clym and Thomasin cannot participate in it due to their personal problems. But all the rustics including Diggory Venn jovially join in this revelry. It transparently authenticates the fact that though Hardy's protagonists are psychologically daunted by the tragedies of their earthly existence (Mrs. Yeobright has passed away bitten by an adder, Wildeve and Eustacia have been drowned, Clym and Thomasin are much affected by such accidents), the ordinary rustics, though bitten regularly by the adder of hardship and drowned in the sea of problems, manifest extraordinary hilarity whenever life offers them such merry occasions. Bakhtin's comment on 'death' in Rabelais's novel seems illuminating in this context:

> In Rabelais's novel the image of death is devoid of all tragic and terrifying overtones. Death is the necessary link in the process of the people's growth and renewal. It is the 'other side' of birth. [*Rabelais and His World* 407]

The last chapter titled 'Cheerfulness Again Asserts Itself at Blooms End, and Clym Finds His Vocation' delineates the happy union of Diggory and Thomasin and the rustics' cheerful participation in it. The rural ambience is always exhilarated by any nuptial, they not only long for its accompanying merriment, but also involve themselves in the preparation how they can entertain the newly-wedded couple and other guests in the best probable manner.

The twenty-fifth of June has been scheduled to be the wedding day of Venn and Thomasin. The novel is terminating, after all, in a happy and jovial note. However, originally Hardy planned to retain Venn as an isolated and mysterious figure who was to disappear from the heath and Thomasin was to remain a widow. But the novelist altered his plot in favour of public opinion.

On the scheduled day Grandfer Cantle, Humphrey, Fairway and some other rustics engage themselves to make a feather-bed, the proposed marriage gift for the couple. The Grandfer, in his usual fervour, designs to present a wedding song called 'Down in Cupid's Gardens' that night. Soon a coach carrying the newly married couple is driven past them and with a 'Hurrah!' they wave their hands to congratulate them and 'Grandfer Cantle's seals dancing merrily in the sunlight as he twirled himself about' (*RN* 311).

In the evening all the invitees assemble to celebrate the wedding. Mr. Venn asks Christian to sing and as usual, the diffident young man moves about in his chair seeming afraid at the request and 'his father struck up a stave instead of him' (*RN* 313). The guests hold up their glasses and drink the married couples' health. Thus the rural congregation celebrate the occasion in a jaunty manner. To go back to Bakhtin once again, "Carnival celebrates the destruction of the old and the birth of the new world—the new year, the new spring, the new kingdom" [*Rabelais and His World* 410].

NOTE

1. This subversive attitude of the rural bystanders may also be seen in the light of Hardy's loss of faith in religion: 'By the age of twenty-seven he had already lost her faith' (Cecil 22). This was caused by the Darwinian theory of evolution which shook the rational psyche of the novelist, mid-nineteenth century criticism of the Bible and other such influences.

WORKS CITED

Bakhtin, Mikhail. *Rabelais and His World* (translated by Helene Iswolsky). Bloomington: Indiana University Press, 1984.

Bloom, Harold (ed.). *Thomas Hardy: Modern Critical Views*. New York: Chelsea House Publishers, 1987.

Brown, Douglas. *Thomas Hardy*. London: Longmans; Green and Co. Ltd., 1967.

Bullen, J.B. *The Expressive Eye: Fiction and Perception in the Work of Thomas Hardy*. Oxford: Clarendon Press, 1986.

Butler, Lance John. *Thomas Hardy*. Cambridge: Cambridge University Press, 1977.

Gregor, Ian. *The Great Web*. London: Faber and Faber, 1974.

Hardy, Thomas. *The Return of the Native*. New York: W.W. Norton & Company, 1969. Page numbers of textual references are given in brackets. Referred to as *RN*.

Millgate, Michael. *Thomas Hardy: A Biography*. Oxford: Clarendon Press, 1992.

Palgrave, F.T. *The Golden Treasury*. New York: The New American Library, 1961.

Pinion, F.B. *A Hardy Companion*. London: Macmillan Press Ltd., 1977.

Rutland, William R. *Thomas Hardy: A Study of His Writings and Their Background*. New York: Russel & Russel Inc., 1962.

Turner, Paul D.L. *The Life of Thomas Hardy*. Oxford: Blackwell Publishers, 2001.

Incorporated Styles in Virginia Woolf's Short Stories

BEHZAD POURGHARIB

ONE of Woolf's recurring concerns through the totality of her critical work is consciousness, the flux of character and the success of novelistic discourse in either capturing or evading these issues. Along with fictional techniques of characterization, Woolf also scrutinizes constructs of feminity in patriarchal society and the language and style of women novelists in a convention—bound literary sphere. These issues—of character, of consciousness, of women and of literary language—are the components in the body of Woolf's critical thought and literary practice. When viewed in conjunction with each other, these components display their own brand of dialogism.

When Woolf writes, "that an ordinary mind on an ordinary day [...] receives a myriad impressions [...] an incessant shower of innumerable atoms," she is declaring consciousness to be an ambiguous flux. Such a critical assertion in "Modern Fiction" and other essays is accompanied by Woolf's actual portrayal of consciousness in her fiction. In her novels and short stories, inner speech is an amalgamation of other's words and of social discourses. Thus the character's utterance in Woolf's fiction is in dialogue with other voices, and is in a state of ambiguous uncertainty. Thus one basic element in Woolf's critical writing is the awareness of voices and ideologies which determine the tone and style of speech. She incorporates this perception into her fiction. This phenomenon points out to the context, either literary-artistic or socio-cultural, which gives rise to these multiple voices. From this premise, we can go one step further to Bakhtin's theory of heteroglossia.

Heteroglossia is a phenomenon which indicates the various language styles and genres of speech and writing that exist within a national vernacular. This stylistic stratification finds voice in the novelistic from which permits the simultaneous existence of the style and discourse of the author/narrator and of others. One stylistic means of introducing heteroglossia into fiction is through the "novelistic image" or "the image of a language." This means that the author uses a language that is not his own in order to exhibit its style as well as its ideological structure. Moreover the author may well be opposed to this style and its goals. Such a confrontation between styles can be noted in Virginia Woolf's short stories.

In this paper, "stylistic dialogue," rather than the dialogue of single voices is examined in four short stories by Virginia Woolf. Bakhtin's concept of heteroglossia explains this phenomenon. Heteroglossia "is a description of stylistic and generic stratification and conflict within the confines of a national vernacular" (Hirschkop 3). It implies the different language style within a national language, the contexts from which they emerge and the goals they embody.

> All languages of heteroglossia, whatever the principle underlying them and making each unique, are specific points of view on the world, forms for conceptualizing the world in words, specific world-views, each characterized by its own objects, meanings and values. As such they all may be juxtaposed to one another and be interrelated dialogically [...] they are all able to enter into the unitary plane of the novel, which can unite in itself parodic stylizations of generic languages, various forms of stylizations and illustrations of professional and period—bound languages, the languages of particular generations, of social dialects and others [...]. They may all be drawn up by the novelist for the orchestration of his themes, and for the refracted (indirect) expression of his intentions and values. (Bakhtin, *Discourse in the Novel* 291-92)

Any of these language styles enter into the novel through the "novelistic image" or "the image of a language," whereby the author represents a particular style that is not his own. It "is not simply an example of it but an exhibition of its spirit its ideological structure" (Hirschkop 32).

Dialogism in this chapter will be viewed as the need of each form of speech to position itself stylistically among other forms of speech. In the stories, the language of dreams, the subconscious, and fantasy, is in dialogue with the language of waking—consciousness and everyday reality. The changing language styles are represented through "novelistic images." These novelistic images do not carry the narrator's intentions directly, but refract them, and create double-voiced discourse. The dialogic element is evident in stylistic parody through novelistic images, humorous quips directed at another's word, contrasting styles and negations. In these stories, dialogism or polyphony is seen less as the relation between individual utterances and more as the "confrontation between social conventions of style or genre" (Hirschkop 11).

Such a confrontation between styles can be noted in "Mr. Bennett and Mrs. Brown"[1] Virginia Woolf represents the language of the Realists and so reveals their ideology, intentions and views, which are in contrast to her own. Realistic ideology, Woolf protests, is superficial and chauvinistic. Moreover the realistic conventions governing the literature of male writers such as Bennett, Galsworthy and Wells are inadequate to the expression of certain unacknowledged aspects of reality and approaches to character. Woolf also implies that the understanding and depiction of feminity eludes these patriarchal writers. She wishes to replace their language style with its concomitant view of the world, of novels and character representation, with her own language, style and views. When approached by the fledgling writer Woolf, for advice about describing human nature represented by Mrs. Brown, the Realists say:

> Begin by saying that her father kept a shop in Harrogate. Ascertain the rent. Ascertain the wages of the shop assistants in the year 1878. Discover what her mother died of. Describe cancer. Describe calico. Describe [...]. (Woolf, "Mr. Bennett and Mrs. Brown" 109)

After having parodied the language of the Realists, Woolf rejects it outright: "But I cried 'Stop! Stop! And I regret to say that I threw that ugly, that clumsy, that incongruous tool out of the window" (Woolf, "Mr. Bennett and Mrs. Brown" 109).

Woolf similarly protests against these conventions of plot and form in "Modern Fiction."[2] She represents these conventions of plot and form, through "the image of Realist language," which her irony effectively undermines. Her desire for a different kind of novel writing is refracted through her ironic comments:

> Whether we call it life or spirit, truth or reality, this, the essential thing has moved off, or on, and refuses to be contained any longer in such ill-fitting vestments as we provide. Nevertheless, we go on persevering, conscientiously, constructing our two and thirty chapters after a design which more and more ceases to resemble the vision in our minds. So much of the enormous labour of proving the solidity, the likeliness to life, of the story is not extent of obscuring and

> blotting out the light of the conception. The writer seems constrained, not by his own free will but by some powerful and unscrupulous tyrant who has him in thrall, to provide a plot, to provide comedy, tragedy, love interest, and an air of probability embalming the whole so impeccably that if his figures down to the last button of their coats in the fashion of the hour. The tyrant is obeyed; the novel is done to a turn. ("Modern Fiction" 88)

Woolf represents the literary dictums of the Realists which are "to provide plot, character and two and thirty chapters after a design." She portrays the language of the Realists through the "image of their language" which demands "the air of impeccability and probability in the figures" who are "dressed down to the last button of their coats in the fashion of the hour." She undermines this language which she makes into an object of study and satire. Her own views and her own language see Realistic characters as mere "figures" who are lifeless and must therefore be "embalmed." She satirizes "the enormous labour of providing the solidity, the likeness to life" of the Realist writers.

The stylistic debate which Woolf started in her two famous essays is enacted in the following short stories. Realist conventions of style and genre as Woolf writes in "Mr. Bennett and Mrs. Brown" and in "Modern Fiction" are part of the masculine narrative techniques. As Phyllis Rose comments:

> The novel of the certainties, firm characters in a firm setting, a plot solidity in the hands of an omniscient narrator, the novel which relied for its impact on moral certainties as well […] this kind of novel was masculine. Certainty and stability played little part in Woolf's sense of herself, and it was on her sense of herself that she predicated the new form of the novel: Shifting, subjective, unassertive in its moral stance, it would impose no rigid thirty-two chapters on experience, but would let the emphasis fall where it might. Authority, the rigid imposition of form upon matter, whether the matter be subject peoples or the fictive stuff of life is associated for Woolf with masculinity. (100)

Phyllis Rose goes on to propose that modernist narrative techniques, by virtue of their open-endedness, and ambiguous boundaries, are in some senses feminine. "One could therefore characterize the innovations in the early twentieth century novels as the feminization of fiction" (101).

It is Woolf's chosen task to rewrite the discourse of the novel, as also of feminity. In both literature and life, men and women have different measuring rods, as she remarks in "Women and Fiction":

> It is probable, however, that both in life and in art the values of a woman are not the values of a man. Thus when a woman comes to write a novel, she will find that she is perpetually wishing to alter the established values—to make serious what appears insignificant to a man, and trivial what is important to him. (81)

Changes in the ideological impetus of the novel, the move from outer to inner, result in a language that is different. In the following examination of four short stories, Realistic language is represented and shown in dialogic conflict with non Realistic languages and modes. Literary modes and styles such as Romanticism, Realism, Fantasy and Fable, coexist within the stories. For example, the narrator represents a Romantic style, only to parody it. In another instance, stylistic and thematic connections and contrasts reveal the self-consciousness of a style and its relation to other variations. Thus double-voiced discourse is created.

In two stories, fantasy and fable are narrated through double-voiced discourses: The narrator speaks the language of fable and desire, "with one eye on" the opposing discourse of Rationalism. There is humour due to the narrator's consciousness of two modes of narrative reality—fact and fantasy. Thus the texts are dialogic in terms of the stylistic representation of another's language and ideology through "the image of this language." These images are not the author's yet their language refracts Woolf's intentions.

"A Woman's College from Outside"[3] contains two broad strains of discursive fields. On the one hand there is the discourse of Romanticism, moving into a celebration of indiscipline and finally of feminine unconscious anarchy. In constant dialogue with these discourses are the parodic comments on narrative language, the language of institutionalized discipline and the language of conscious and quotidian concerns.

The two groups of discourses in the story are fundamentally opposed on one point—the notion of the self. The romanticist discourses celebrate the self, and the anti-romanticist discourses through parodies of speech genres and parodic repetitions of phrases, stylistically undermine this celebration of the poetic and inner self. In the first paragraph of the story, parody initiates a dialogue between two classes of discourse—Romantic and Realistic. The world-views these discourses represent are also in conflict. The story opens with a Romantic description of the place:

> The feathery white moon never let the sky grow dark; all night long the chestnut blossoms were white in the green, and dim was the cow-parsley in the meadows. (Woolf, "A Woman's College from Outside" 139)

The stock description of the full moon places the piece in the realm of the poetic. In addition to this is the use of the adjective "white" as an activity of the chestnut blossoms which are seen in the "act" of being white; the last segment of the sentence inverts the syntax in the manner of poetry; "and dim was the cow-parsley in the meadow." The opening description of the moonlit night is denied by the next sentence in which the speaker subverts the impression of the first sentence. This is not an exotic setting in the manner of Romantic literature, the speaker seems to be saying, but merely Cambridge, England:

> Neither to Tartary nor to Arabia went the wind of the Cambridge Courts, but lapsed dreamily in the midst of the grey-blue clouds over the roofs of Newnham. (Woolf, "A Woman's College from Outside" 139)

Foreign lands, which appear in later Romantic poetry, are referred to ironically, so that the introductory sentence is no longer taken to be the direct statement of the author. The first sentence with its images written in a poetic idiom is in *intonational quotation marks*. Its speaking voice is not specified nor indicated by typographical quote marks, but its tone which is poetic and lyrical is not that of the ironic self-conscious speaker of the second sentence. The image of the moonlit night in the first sentence is what defines as a novelistic image.

> Novelistic image: the image of another's language, in the given instance of another's poetic style (sentimental and romantic). The poetic metaphors in these lines [...] in no way function here as the *primary means of representation* [...] rather they themselves have become the object of representation, or more precisely of a representation that is parodied and stylized. The novelistic image of another's style (with the direct metaphors that it incorporates) must be taken in *intonational quotation marks* within the system of direct authorial speech (postulated by us here), that is, taken as if the image were parodic and ironic. (Bakhtin, "From the Prehistory of Novelistic Discourse" 147)

The image of the moonlit night not only describes the night, but also exemplifies the languages, the world-view, and the ideological intention of a person who is not the author. Subsequently too in the story, the representation of discourses like Romanticism, through intonational quotation marks, displays the author's ideological distance from these discourses, as we will demonstrate.

Thus two voices, speaking in close proximity with each other are established in the first two sentences. Ostensibly they speak about the night which is the referential object of their utterances. The second speaker however, also comments on the Romantic imagery, style and world-view of the first speaker and questions the validity of these. In this story, there is parodic repetition of phrases in different contexts and with contrary implications. It is this parody which creates the awareness that the language styles being used in the story are not the author's direct word. This can be noted in the following Romanticized description of Angela and its consequent subversion:

> How bright Angela was, and how bright came back the reflection of herself from the square glass. The whole of her was perfectly delineated perhaps the soul [...] the bright picture hung in the heart of night, the shrine hollowed in the nocturnal blackness. Strange indeed to have the visible proof of the rightness of things; this lily floating flawless upon Time's pool, fearless, as if this were sufficient—this reflection. (Woolf, "A Woman's College from Outside" 139)

The seraphic description of Angela's reflection in the mirror is a romantic vision of the spiritual and aesthetic place of the human being in the world. This description is parodied later by the repetition of the very alliterative phrase—"lily floating, flawless"—that distinguishes it.

> Angella Williams was at Newnham for the purpose of earning her living and could not forget even in moments of impassioned adoration the cheques of her father at Swansea; her mother washing in the scullery; pink frocks out to dry on the line; tokens that even the lily no longer floats flawless upon the pool, but has a name on a card like another. (Woolf, "A Woman's College from Outside" 139)

In the above citations, we have two voices, one attempting to alter, falsify and replace the image of the world produced by the other. Parody is used here as a means of effecting a discursive link between the sublime and mundane, by demonstrating how the sublime is rooted in the ordinary—the lily who "floats flawless upon time's pool," is in fact the offspring of a lower middle class Swansea family.

The thematic content, style and compositional structure of the romanticized speech genres reflect a world-view in which the human being has an eminent place. The goals of Romanticism are to heighten the individual, and to render extraordinary and unique, subjective experiences. These goals are then questioned by the prosaic voice which situates the human being, in this case Angela, in the everyday world. Thus the boundaries of the Romantic vision are extended.

In the examples cited, the same phrase has been used by two speakers in a dialogue. They express different, yet interrelated goals through the repetition of the same linguistic structure, creating a richly double-voiced textual fabric. As Ken Hirschkop comments, "dialogism is only perceptible in specific textual moments, when linguistic structure—syntactic, lexical or generic—appears as the expression of a particular delimited 'point of view' (9).

In this story, the language of Romantic poetry is allied to the language of the anarchic subconscious and finally to discourse of unknown feminity. This is because all three discourses are in some way concerned with the uniqueness of the self. On the other hand, the prosaic, parodying voice continues as a conflicting discourse of discipline, of the conscious self and of patriarchal worldly concerns. These discourses reduce the subject to a cog in the social and patriarchal wheel. Thus a dialogue arises between the language styles of the two sets of narrators. The aspirations of the "poetic-feminine" voice and "realistic-masculine" voice pull in opposite directions. For the poetic voice, as we have shown, seeks to convey the beauty of the night and the metaphysical meaning of life. The parodying realistic voice on the other hand depicts the facts of reality and does so by subverting poetic languages.

The everyday reality of life in the woman's college is the domain of the realistic narrator. This waking life is one of discipline and rules and it depersonalizes its students to "names on cards." The female residents of the college are reduced to a homogeneous collective group whose only purpose is to "rise martially should there be a call, to extinguish a fire, suppress an insurrection, or pass an examination" (Woolf, "A Woman's College from Outside" 141). The rules of the college also suppress feminity and exert sexual neutrality over its student: "We are not eunuchs," one of the students protests.

In contrast to the discourse which reinforces authoritarian disciplines, is the carnivalesque laughter, which disregards "hours, rules, discipline." This feminine laughter gains strength from the metaphors of snow, and wind used to describe it: "Fire, insurrection, examination were all snowed under by laughter, or softly uprooted, the sound seeming to bubble up from the depths and gently waft away the hour, rules, discipline" (Woolf, "A Woman's College from Outside" 140). The parodic repetition of the phrase "extinguish a fire, suppress an insurrection or pass an examination" subverts disciplinarian language and replaces it with anarchic language.

The laughter gains supernatural strength in Bertha's dream where it delineates a world that is exclusive to women; this feminine domain is an underground, night time world, invisible to the outer eye and repressed by the conscious mind.

> The laughter (for she dozed now) floated out much like mist and attached itself by soft elastic shreds to plants and bushes so that the garden was vaporous and clouded. And then swept by the wind, the bushes would bow themselves and the white vapour blow off across the world.
>
> From all the rooms where women slept this vapour issued [...] pouring forth into the garden this bubbling laughter; this laughter of mind and body floating away rules, hours, discipline, immensely fertilizing yet formless, chaotic trailing and straying and tufting the rose bushes with shreds of vapour. (Woolf, "A Woman's College from Outside" 141)

The surrealistic dream sequence is thematically powerful in relation to the rest of the short story. It is a flight into a subconscious and archetypal feminine reality. It is also powerful because it is not in intonational quotation marks, for there is no linguistic parody or ideological subversion. It is, therefore, not another's language through which the author expresses her intention, but the author's direct word. The Romanticized notion of the self—"Lily floating flawless upon time's pool, fearless"—is an easy target of parody. The anarchic laughter of the feminine self is not; instead it is a carnivalesque parody of discipline.

With regard to the idea of carnival, Bakhtin describes "the fully articulated superstructure of laughter, erected over all serious straight-forward genres [...] the tendency toward a laughing double for every serious from" ("From the Prehistory of Novelistic Discourse" 153). In the story the disruptive feminine laughter which appears as a dream, is the carnivalesque answer to the masculine discourse of education and discipline which is imposed by the college on its students. Nancy glazener comments on Bakhtin's carnivalesque mode:

> Carnival laughter challenges traditional concepts of logic and identify. It is ambivalent in that it affirms and denies at once, diminishing the individual but re-ennobling him on her through the medium of the collectivity. (113)

The discourse of discipline reduces students to "names on cards" who can only act collectively with a predetermined purpose. The discourse of indiscipline in the story does not confer individuality *per se*. Rather it unifies the mind and body and is holistic. Since it reaches its apogee in the dream, this discourse inevitably leads to psychoanalytical dilemmas about the self and consciousness.

The disunification within the psyche at the moment of the commencement of the castration complex is intrinsic to psychoanalytical thought. It is interesting that Juliet Mitchell links the undivided child to the carnivalesque mode.

> The moment of the castration complex, the moment when the heterogeneously sexual, polymorphously perverse, carnivalesque child has imposed on it the division of 'the law; the one law; the law of patriarchy.' (426)

The unification of mind any body in Berha's dream is akin to the psychic unification which is the psychoanalytic ideal. In this story, the initial parody of Romantic language and its concomitant notion of the self are subsequently inverted. This inversion occurs when parody is directed against the prosaic Realistic word, which is reduced to ineffectuality by the feminine subconscious self. Bertha's dream-vision of primordial feminine laughter links the discourse of psychoanalysis, feminism and Romanticism. The connection between modern Psychology and Romantic individualism has also been drawn by Lionel Trilling.

> For Psychoanalysis is one of the culminations of the Romanticist literature of the nineteenth century [...] this literature, despite its avowals, was itself scientific in at least the sense of being passionately devoted to a research into the self. (276)

Approaches to the self, both objective and subjective, are seen in this story as well as in "In the Orchard."[4] Susan Dick notes the connection in Virginia Woolf's mind between "A Woman's College from Outside" and "In the Orchard" (published in 1923): "Virginia Woolf's reference to Angela as "Miranda" four times in the holograph and once in the typescript suggest a link between the young woman in this story and Miranda in "In the Orchard."

The dialogue between the Realist and Romanticist literary conventions in "Woman's College" continues with alterations, in "In the Orchard." Here too the cultural context and approaches to the self are raised by and within the representing language. "In the Orchard" is an experiment in different ways of seeing and linguistically representing the same event. It is divided typographically into three sections and each has the same frame or story line: Miranda falls asleep and awakens in the orchard. This frame is fleshed out in a realistic manner by an omniscient narrator in Section I. The interpretation in Section II is through Miranda's daydreams which are shown as being false in the light of the first section. This in itself is a source of conflict between the two sections and creates a dialogue which is carried on in Section III, which veers sharply away from the Realism of Section I. Section III breaks new ground by rendering the human element of the previous two sections insignificant in a humorous manner. It is a visually impressionistic section which sees the orchard as a place of lines, planes and spheres.

The differing viewpoints and language styles of the three sections embody different, perhaps contradictory ideological goals. What cannot be ignored is that though each section is a repetition, it also is a change of focus within the same outer frame. The unchanging outer structure of the three sections ensures that even though each section is a different interpretation, the individual narrative cannot but be conscious of the other narrative focuses in the short story. As Hirschkop writes: "one represents discourse for some definite purpose; it will only be against the backcloth of a certain story one wants to tell that represented speech will become the image of a language" (23).

Section I of "In the Orchard" is a display of the masculine, Realist impetus which Woolf deplores in "Mr. Bennett and Mrs. Brown" and "Modern Fiction." As the ensuing analysis shows, Section I is countered by Sections II and III through "feminine" narrative techniques. Section I seems to be the exact version of the truth because of the wide gamut of human life that it takes into account. Thus the narrative follows Realist literary conventions which include descriptions and authoritative judgments on the life of the people surrounding the orchard: The village children "saying the multiplication tables in unison," Old Parsley of the village "blind drunk," the Rector "returning thanks to Heaven for six poor women of the parish" are accounted for. This is accompanied with a description of the countryside surrounding the orchard. Woods, meadows and hills are described while the focaliser ascends physically in space, never losing sight of Miranda. Thus the narrative achieves a wide range of vision.

Facility of value judgments is a privilege of the omniscient narrator. In this section the omniscient narrator delights in Miranda lying asleep in the grass with the breeze "rippling" her purples dress "like a flower attached to a stalk"; He feels pity and scorn for the drunken man and the poor women of the parish; The wind is seen as a titanic monster "eyeless and brainless, meeting nothing that could stand against it," rather than as a natural force. The vision telescopes from grass to winds in a vertical sweep of visual images as well as auditory messages, starting from Miranda lying asleep in the grass up to the wind and back to Miranda.

> Miranda slept in the orchard, lying in a long chair beneath the apple-tree [...]. Four feet in the air over her head [...] there was a shrill clamour (of) the school children saying the multiplication tables in unison [...]. Next there was a solitary try [...] sad, human, brutal. Old Parsley was indeed, blind drunk. Then [...] thirty feet above the earth (the organ) chimed with a pensive and lugubrious note [...]. The sound floated out and was cut into atoms by a flock of fieldfares flying at enormous speed [...] two hundred feet above Miranda lying asleep in the orchard, bells thudded, intermittent, sullen, didactic [...]. And above that with a sharp squeak, the golden feather of the church tower turned from south to east. The wind changed [...] it droned, above the woods, the meadows, the hills [...] Miles below, in a space as big as the eye of a needle, Miranda stood upright and cried aloud: Oh, I shall be late for tea. (Woolf, "In the Orchard" 143-44)

The wide angle of the vision creates an appearance of objectivity and distanced impartiality in the narrator who has the position of mastery. The narrator's role is similar to the prosaic voice of "Woman's College." The narrator here can arbitrarily describe and contain the subject within his languages. His voice seems indisputable. This section has the status of *histoire* or "story" which is the actual events, the truth, in the light of which the other two sections are regarded as individual versions, private and idiosyncratic The authoritative voice of this section, which reports facts and passes judgments, is indisputable. The narrator and focaliser seem to be one, or at least are not ideologically at variance with each other. Thus the picture of the orchard from near and from an eminence is conveyed in a "seamlessly unified" manner in section I.

It is precisely this apparent omniscience and realism against which the next two sections are in conflict. It is true Woolf admits, that as a novelist she is often "in thrall" of "Some powerful and unscrupulous tyrant," who demands that she "provide a plot, to provide comedy, tragedy, love interest and an air of probability" for her writing. The simultaneous representation and revolt against an alien discourse is intrinsic to Woolf's writing. The consciousness of a realist and therefore "true" style of writing impinges on the following sections.

Section II is set against the concrete context established in Section I. It is a record of Miranda's thoughts and shows the discrepancy between these mere daydreams and the "reality" of Section I. Outer sounds such as Miranda's own voice, the children reciting their tables, the teacher rapping Jimmy on his knuckles, the village drunk's cry, the church organ and bells, go either unheeded by her, or if she hears these sounds, they do not have the ordinary meaning with reference to out reality. Outer events of section I are transformed by her imagination into elements in her private world. "[…] when the shout of the drunken man overhead, she drew breath with an extraordinary ecstasy, for she thought that she heard life itself crying out from a rough tongue in a scarlet mouth." (Woolf, "In the Orchard" 144)

Miranda interprets and patterns outer reality:

> Naturally she was being married when the organ played the tune from Hymns Ancient and Modern, and, when the bells rang […] the sullen intermittent thud made her think that the very earth shook with the hoofs of the horse that was galloping towards her […] and it seemed that everything had already begun moving, crying, riding, flying round her, across her, towards her in a pattern. (Woolf, "In the Orchard" 144)

Miranda's daydreams are disproved by the narratorial gloss which speaks from the vantage point of the truth established in the previous section. The narration is double-voiced. It represents Miranda's views and language but remains conscious of the stronger Realistic voice. The narrator and the focaliser, that is Miranda, are not unified. The workings of Miranda's mind though displayed are shown as being false.

There are multiple levels of irony at work. Obvious irony is directed against Miranda's fantasy. However Woolf, who championed the subjectivity of experience, is also subtly undermining the thorough-going materialism of section I. The facility of describing Mrs. Brown's external life—her father's shop Harrowgate, her mother's cancer etc., versus "the appalling effort of saying" what the writer really means is described in "Mr. Bennett and Mrs. Brown." Mrs. Brown protests that she is subtle and indescribable "quite different from what people made out."

In section II of the story, the Reality of I supersedes Miranda's intrinsic voice. As in "Mr. Bennett and Mrs. Brown" the inescapable discourse of Realism frames and falsifies Miranda's personal utterance. Of all three sections, the third best exemplifies the title *In the Orchard*, for it is exclusively about the orchard as a compact world in itself. In fact a novel vision is put forward in this section, partially because of new information and partially because of a novel way of seeing what the previous two sections have described. Thus Miranda in her purple dress is seen in this section as a mere purple streak which slits the green grass.

> Her purple dress stretched between the two apple trees [...] across a corner of the orchard, the blue green was slit by a purple streak. (Woolf, "In the Orchard" 215)

Miranda's dress is seen in spatial relation to the apple trees and in chromatic relation to the grass; but nothing else about the wearer herself is noted. The admirably pretty girl of Section I, the dreamy girl of Section II is reduced here to a dress of purple colour. Since this section is only read in the light of the previous two sections, the diminished importance of Miranda and the increased importance of the apple orchard is a source of quizzical humour. The narrator provides detailed information about the number of apple trees in the orchard and the angle at which they stand. The trees are also seen as having upward movement, as if the focaliser can see the process of their growth before his very eyes.

> There were twenty-four apple trees in the orchard, some slanting slightly, others growing straight with a rush up the trunk which spread into branches and formed into round red or yellow drops. (Woolf, "In the Orchard" 145)

The growth of these trees is connected to the flight of birds:

> A wagtail flew [...]. Cautiously hopping, a thrush advanced [...] a sparrow fluttered just above the grass. The uprush of the trees was tied down by these movements. (Woolf, "In the Orchard" 145)

In this description of threes, and of apples as "round red or yellow drop," we see a departure from cultural codes of literary communication. Codes, according to Barthes, "are certain types of deja-lu (already read), of deja-fait (already done)" (191). In this section the unusual description of nature is a departure from literary codes established in the previous sections. For instance the sky is seen as secondary to the tree; "The sky exactly fitted the leaves." The sky is not seen as a limitless expanse as it was in Section I. Instead it is a tangible material, though of less importance than the orchard itself. The orchard is seen through the eyes of an impressionist painter with a sky framing and enclosing the whole.

In this section the dehumanization of Miranda, the priority given to the trees of the orchard rather than to the human life surrounding it, the diminishing of the vault of the sky to a mere frame for the orchard are ways of contradicting the previous two sections. This subversion, within the same outer framework succeeds in parodying the goals and intentions of Sections I and II. In this story we see a three-fold approach to the same framework—the masculine Realist, the feminine and the experimental. This ensures that each approach is read in the light of the other two approaches. Thus each section, with its opposing ideological impetus and narrative technique, is a commentary on the other two sections, and this device creates dialogic overtones.

The language of Realism and its concomitant approach to the self is represented and denied in the following two stories, with, however, a different approach. "Nurse Lugton's Curtain"[5] and "The Widow and the Parrot: A True Story"[6] are stories written for children, and they use fable and fantasy with comic effect. The apparently serious narrator, who relates the fantastic narrative, is not in fact taken seriously by the reader.

Bakhtin discusses folkloric narrators and storytellers who "recommend themselves as specific and limited verbal ideological points of view, belief systems, opposed to the literary expectations and points of view that constitute the background needed to perceive them [...]. The speech of such narrators is always *another's speech* (as regards the real or potential direct discourse of the author) and in another's language (i.e., insofar as it is a particular variant of the literary language that clashes with the language of the narrator)" (313).

In both stories the fantastic narrator is as much the object of amusement as is the story itself. The author and narrator are not one:

> Behind the narrator's story we read a second story, the author's story; he is the one who tells us how the narrator tells stories, and also tells us about the narrator himself. We acutely sense two levels at each moment in the story; one, the level of the narrator, a belief system filled with his objects, meanings and emotional expressions, and the other, the level of the author, who speaks, albeit in a refracted way, by means of this story and through this story. (314)

"Nurse Lugton's Curtain" was written for Woolf's niece, Ann Stephen, when she was visiting her aunt in the country. As Anne Olivier Bell points out, Virginia Woolf's allusion in her diary to one of the Nurse Lugton's sayings suggests that she "may have had a real existence in the Stephen household" (Oliver Bell, "Notes" 296). Nurse Lugton falls asleep while stitching a blue curtain for Mrs. John Jasper Gingham's drawing room window, and when she snores for the fifth time, the curtain comes to life: "the blue stuff turned to blue air; the trees waved; you could hear the water of the lake breaking" ("Nurse Lugton's Curtain" 153). Nurse Lugton's snores play the role of releasing the creatures printed on the curtain into animation:

> The animals with which it was covered did not move till Nurse Lugton snored for the fifth time. One, two, three, four, five—ah, the old woman was at last asleep. The antelope nodded to zebra, the giraffe bit through the leaf on the tree top; all the animals began to toss and prance. For the pattern on the blue stuff was made of troops of wild beasts and below them was a lake and a bridge and a town with round roofs and little men and women looking out of the windows and riding over the bridge on horseback. ("Nurse Lugton's Curtain" 153)

Discourse in this sketch is humorous because the language of the nursery authority figures. Nurse Lugton is pitted against the language of the make-believe world. Nurse Lugton is an object of amusement because she falls asleep and is rendered unaware. Though she is the enforcer of authority and discipline in the nursery; she has no conscious control over the make-believe world that springs to life on her lap. She is also ridiculous as the epitome of the Victorian nanny who is "mortally afraid of poking through the bars with her umbrella at the Zoo! Even a black beetle made her jump" ("Nurse Lugton's Curtain" 155). Ironically, it is this faint-hearted woman whose apron is "covered with [...] all these wild beasts trampling on it" ("Nurse Lugton's Curtain" 154-55). Thus she cradles what she fears, albeit unconsciously, in her lap.

Similarly, the make-believe world is also an object of amusement. To this world Nurse Lugton is an ogress who has the power to freeze any creature who wanders into her territory. Nurse Lugton has the animals of the second order world in her toils:

> For it was well-known even the smallest monkey was enchanted. For a great ogress had them in her toils, the people knew; and the great ogress was called Lugton [...]. She had a face like the side of a mountain with great precipices and avalanches, and chasms for her eyes and hair and nose and teeth. And every animal which strayed into her territories she froze alive, so that all day they stood stock still on her knee, but when she fell asleep, then they were released and came down in the evening to millamarchamantopolis to drink. ("Nurse Lugton's Curtain" 55)

The magnification of Nurse Lugton's face into a mountain with chasms and precipices by the creatures of the make-believe world is also a source of humour to the reader of the short story. The daily instruments and occurrences of Nurse Lugton's world are the force of nature in this fantasy world. Her golden thimble burns over it like the sun, and her snoring is the sound of the wind roaring through the forest. Again humour is directed against the animals for fearing what the reader known is patently harmless.

The languages of both worlds—that of Nurse Lugton and of the fantasy world—are portrayed. Both languages are satirized. Thus the humour is two-pronged and the author uses both discourses but identifies with neither. Bakhtin comments on how the dialogic tension between languages and belief systems, permits the author to realize his intentions:

> The author is not to be found in the language of the narrator, not in the normal literary language to which the story opposes itself (although a given story may be closer to a given languages)—but rather, the author utilizes now one languages, now another, in order to avoid giving himself up wholly to either of them; he makes use of this

> verbal give-and-take, this dialogue of languages at every point in his work, in order that he himself might remain as it were neutral with regard to languages, a third party in a quarrel between two people (although he might be a biased third party). (314)

The dialogic tension between two language systems is found in "The Widow and the Parrot: A True Story" as well. There is an uneasy coexistence of the natural and supernatural levels of reality in the story. It was written by Woolf in the same period as "Nurse Lugton's Curtain," for her sister Vanessa Bell's children. The discourse of the fable and the contrary discourse of empirical facts are both represented. Neither discourse is the direct word of the author, yet both are needed for the expression of the author's point of view as the analysis shows. The element of the supernatural is essential to the story and is recounted by a narrator whose persona is that of a rationalist, convinced against his will by visual and auditory evidence, that the irrational and the supernatural exist. Thus it is common hearsay that the ghosts of Mrs. Gage the Widow and James the Parrot, still haunt the site of the burned-down house where they discovered the miser's treasure one hundred years ago.

> It is commonly said that if you visit it (the site of the burned-down house) in the moonlight, you may hear a parrot tapping with his beak upon the brick floor, while others have seen an old woman sitting there in a white apron. (Woolf, "The Widow and the Parrot: A True Story" 163)

In the story, Mrs. Gage is shown as a kind-hearted woman who takes pity on the parrot whose feathers are "sadly neglected." She decides that he is either "unhappy" or "hungry," and offers him a piece of sugar "saying in a very kind tone [...] that she would see to it that he was as happy as a bird could be" (Woolf, "The Widow and the Parrot: A True Story" 15). It is because of her kindness that she earns the gratitude of the parrot who save her life and shows her the buried treasure.

The theme of the grateful animal/tree/object who was the power to reward a deserving person materially is intrinsic to fantasy. So too is the image of the dumb beast who has the power to foresee events and prevent death. In the story the widow keeps the facts of the parrot's supernatural powers secret and only reveals them on her death-bed to the clergyman. He plays the role of the "reliable witness" and encourages the narrator to entertain, if not accept, the supernatural story:

> It was not till she lay on her death bed that she told the clergyman [...] the whole story, adding that she was quite sure that the house had been burnt on purpose by the parrot James who being aware of her danger on the river bank, flew into the scullery and upset the oil stove which was keeping some scraps warm for her dinner. By this act, he not only saved her from drowning, but brought to light the three thousand pounds, which could have been found in no other manner. Such, she said is the reward of kindness to animals. (Woolf, "The Widow and the Parrot: A True Story" 163)

The narrator of the story speaks a discourse that is double-voiced—this is because he supports the language and presuppositions of the supernatural, yet must speak as a sceptic to a rational audience. The notion of a supernatural bond between the parrot and the widow is put forward by the "impartial" narrator, along with evidence to support it. When Mrs. Gage makes her dying confession, "The Clergyman thought that she was wandering in her mind. But it is certain that the very moment the breath was out of her body, James the parrot shrieked out, "Not at home! Not at home!" and fell off his perch, stone dead." (Woolf, "The Widow and the Parrot: A True Story" 163)

In this story there are two levels in terms of intention of the speaker towards the purported addressee or listener. One intention is to sustain the conditions of the supernatural world by using the fable narrative. Another, perhaps contrary intention, is to maintain a distanced impartiality towards the fantastic events so that the sceptic and the rational among the readers will not entirely disbelieve the fantasy. These dual intentions of the narrator result in the use of differing narrative and stylistic devices.

On the one hand the story uses elements of the fable such as a miser's hoard which is revealed to a poor widow after her act of kindness to a parrot; the supernatural bond which exists between the mistress and her pet is also part of the fable plot. On the other hand are the narrative devices of giving rational proof and factual evidence such as the clergyman's testimony, what people see and hear on the site of the burned-down house etc. These are "stylistic" devices which belong to the rational intentions of the narrator.

The landmarks of Virginia Woolf's contemporary world are also incorporated into the story: Monks House at Rodmell and "Asheham House, lately the seat of Leonard Woolf" (Woolf, "The Widow and the Parrot: A True Story" 159), are locations within the fable. This device creates a complicity between Woolf and her intended reader i.e., her nephews and niece.[7] There is also a gap in time between the events of the story and the current time:

> In those days, I must tell you, there was no bridge over the river at Southease, nor had the road to Newham yet been made. To reach Rodmell it was necessary to cross the River Ouse, by a ford, traces of which still exist, but this could only be attempted at low tide, when the stones on the river bed appeared above the water. (Woolf, "The Widow and the Parrot: A True Story" 156-57)

Thus the distance of time and the familiarity of the physical setting also lend credibility to the fable.

Commenting on women writers' use of fantasy in her chapter on "Myths Dreams and Nightmares," Flora Alexander writes that there are substantial areas of human experience that cannot be approached by methods of social realism and require that the illusion of everyday reality should be suspended. Fantasy, she writes, "does not mean something whimsical or created in a random escapist way. Rather it indicates a mode in which dreams, or metaphors, are employed to say something about social and historical or psychological realities" (61). In the case of the two supernatural stories, the languages of fantasy and fact clash in their attempts to discredit the other. The narrator subscribes to fantasy, yet cannot overtly show it. This role is yet another expression of Woolf's battle with Realist literary language and conventions.

Both stories generate a humour that is two-pronged. In the first, both Nurse Lugton and the fantasy world are a source of humour. In "The Widow and the Parrot," there is good-natured amusement directed at the character Mrs Gage, and her language. Laughter is also inflected in all of the narrator's attempts to justify the irrational world to the rational mind. Paradoxically, the narrator supports the supernatural with the discourse of materialism.

Virginia Woolf represents the language of Fantasy and of Factual evidence, expresses her ideas through them and yet reveals their limitation and insufficiencies. As Bakhtin writes, "It is, after all, precisely in the light of another potential language or style that a given straightforward style is parodied, travestied, ridiculed" (139).

Fantasy cannot sustain itself in the light of Modern Scientific thought. Yet, in "The Widow and the Parrot" it exists in tandem with the prerequisites to rational belief, that is visual, auditory and tactile proofs; these proofs lend the fable credence. Thus the rational element which in itself is the contrary of the irrational, is used by the narrator to support what it, by definition denies. The various styles represented and/or parodied in "A Woman's College from Outside" are concerned with views on the self. The debate carried out is biased in favour of the unconscious feminine collectivity rather than a conscious masculine homogeneity. This debate is linguistically represented through parodic repetitions and stylizations which allow the author to represent language styles without identifying with them. This technique of author-distantiation is forcefully repeated in "In the Orchard." Here, the three conflicting sections represent three different language styles and ideologies. Objective realism and subjective fantasy are opposed in Sections I and II and the objective satirizes the subjective. The former's conventionality is, however, parodied in Section III which subverts the language and authoritative descriptions of Section I. Yet it is not possible to determine any section as the truth with which the author fully identifies.

The last two stories—"Nurse Lugton's Curtain" and "The Widow and the Parrot: A True Story," move away from ideologies about the self, yet continue the debate on linguistic conventions of Realism and discourses which "defy" Realism. Here parody and humour serve to expand the notion of Realism to include realms that it would normally deny.

Virginia Woolf's representation of the language of Bennett Wells and Galsworthy and her simultaneous rejection of such language is symptomatic of her writing. In the stories examined above, she represents another's language and outlook through, "novelistic images." Though she does not identify with these languages, they are used to convey her intentions, obliquely. Moreover, her intentions are not fixed—the identification with any one point of view is not complete. This is because the criticism of the novelistic image, which includes a language style and a world-view, comes from within the image itself.

NOTES

1. Virginia Woolf, "Mr. Bennett and Mrs. Brown," *Essays*, ed. Walter James. London: Chatto and Windus, 1966.
2. Virginia Woolf, "Modern Fiction," *Twentieth Century Criticism: A Reader*, ed. David Lodge. London: Longman, 1972.
3. Virginia Woolf, "A Woman's College from Outside," *The Complete Shorter Fiction of Virginia Woolf*, ed. Susan Dick. London: Hogarth, 1985. Susan

Dick notes that the draft of this story is located in the first holograph of *Jacob's Room*, "thus suggesting that V.W. was still planning to use it in *Jacob's Room*. The chapter was not included in the novel, however, but was published in November 1926 as *A Woman's College from Outside* in *Atlanta's Garland: Being the Book of the Edinburgh University Women's Union*" (295). Citations form the text will be indicated with page numbers in parentheses.

4. Virginia Woolf, "In the Orchard," *The Complete Shorter Fiction of Virginia Woolf*, ed. Susan Dick. Citations from the story will be indicated in page numbers in parentheses in this chapter.
5. Virginia Woolf, "Nurse Lugton's Curtain," *The Complete Shorter Fiction of Virginia Woolf*, ed. Susan Dick. Citations from the text will be indicated with page numbers in parentheses.
6. Virginia Woolf, "The Widow and the Parrot: A True Story," *The Complete Short Fiction of Virginia Woolf*, ed. Susan Dick. Susan Dick notes that this short story "first appeared in *The Charleston Bulletin*, a newspaper produced by the Bell children at Charleston in the 1920's. Citations from the story will be indicated with page numbers in parentheses.
7. Susan Dick notes that the landmarks in the story are those of Woolf's own life: "VW invested her 'true' story with local colour by placing the widow's brother's house near Monk's house, the house in the village in Rodmell where the Woolf's moved when they left Asheham in the September of 1919."

WORKS CITED

Bakhtin, M.M. *Discourse in the Novel, the Dialogic Imagination: Four Essays*, trans. Emerson, Caryl and Michael Holquist, ed. Michael Holquist. Austin: University of Texas Press, 1981.

——. "From the Prehistory of Novelistic Discourse." *Modern Criticism and Theory: A Reader*, ed. David Lodge. London: Longman, 1988.

Barthes, Roland. "Textual Analysis: Poe's Valdemar," *Modern Criticism and Theory: A Reader*, ed. David Lodge. London: Longman, 1977.

Alexander, Flora. "Myths, Dreams and Nightmares." *Contemporary Women Novelists*. London: Edward Arnold, 1989.

Glazener, Nancy. "Dialogic Subversions: Bakhtin, the Novel and Gertrude Stein," *Bakhtin and Cultural Theory*, eds. Ken Hirschkop and David Shepherd. Manchester: Manchester U.P., 1989.

Hirschkop, Ken. "Introduction," *Bakhtin and Cultural Theory*, eds. Ken Hirschkop and David Shepherd. Manchester: Manchester U.P., 1989.

Mitchell, Juliet. "Feminity, Narrative and Psychoanalysis," *Modern Criticism and Theory: A Reader*, ed. David Lodge. Longman, 1988.

Oliver Bell, Anne. "Notes" in *The Complete Short Shorter Fiction of Virginia Woolf*, ed. Susan Dick. New York: Harcourt Brace Jovanovich, 1985.

Phyllis Rose, *Woman of Letters: A Life of Virginia Woolf.* London: Routledge and Kegan Paul, 1978.

Trilling, Lionel. "Freud and Literature," *Twentieth Century Criticism: A Reader*, ed. David Lodge. London: Longman, 1972.

Woolf, Virginia. "Mr. Bennett and Mrs. Brown," *Selections from her Essays*, ed. Walter James. London: Chatto and Windus, 1966.

——. "Modern Fiction," *Twentieth Century Criticism: A Reader*, ed. David Lodge. London: Longman, 1972.

——. "Women and Fiction," *Granite and Rainbow*. London: Hogarth Press, 1981.

——. "A Woman's College from Outside," *The Complete Shorter Fiction of Virginia Woolf*, ed. Susan Dick. London: Hogarth, 1985.

❑❑❑

Statement about Ownership and other Particulars of
The Atlantic Critical Review

FORM IV (See Rule 8)

Place of Publication	:	New Delhi
Periodicity of the Publication	:	Quarterly
Printer's Name	:	Manish Kumar
Nationality	:	Indian
Address	:	B-2, Vishal Enclave, New Delhi 110027
Publisher's Name	:	Manish Kumar
Nationality	:	Indian
Address	:	B-2, Vishal Enclave, New Delhi 110027
Editor's Name	:	Mohit K. Ray
Nationality	:	Indian
Address	:	77, Green Park, Burdwan, West Bengal-713104
Names and addresses of individuals who own the newspaper and partners or shareholders holding more than one per cent of the total capital	:	K.R. Gupta B-2, Vishal Enclave New Delhi-110027

I, Manish Kumar, hereby declare that the particulars given above are true to the best of my knowledge and belief.

Sd/-

Date : 1st April, 2007

MANISH KUMAR
Publisher

Mothers and Children in Two Poems by Mina Loy

PILAR SÁNCHEZ CALLE

IN recent years, the neglected modernist poet Mina Loy (London, 1882; Aspen, Colorado, 1966) has been rediscovered by a new generation of readers. Mina Loy grew up in London and in 1900 she went to Berlin and later on to Paris to study art. She left Paris for Florence in 1906, where she lived for ten years with her first husband and two children. Loy travelled to New York in 1916, becoming very active in the city's avant-garde scene. She came back to Europe in 1918, living in London and Italy till she moved to Paris in 1921. In 1936, Loy settled definitively in the United States, first in Manhattan and then in Aspen, Colorado, where she died in 1966. Her poems were praised by Ezra Pound (he coined the term "logopoeia" to describe them) and admired and eagerly read by many others such as William Carlos Williams, Hart Crane and E.E. Cummings. However, printed in little magazines or published by small publishing houses, Loy's work was lost to later reading audiences, perhaps because she did not publish anything between 1931 and 1944. Among the reasons for this absence of published work we can mention her poems' technical experimentation and, above all, a subject matter based in female experience and located itself in the female body (Benstock 387). Mina Loy's poetry was unlike that of any other woman poet of her generation. She used free verse with an audacious spacing of her lines and chose simultaneity and the juxtaposition of disparate elements to question conventional contexts of meaning (Ress 119). Her poems see art, love, sex, and childbirth from the point of view of a "new woman" (Burke 1997: v-vi). When dealing with the body, Loy exhibits a vocabulary of eroticism which revels in the body functions, concentrating on its skin, tissue and fluids as ways of figuring love. Loy does not idealize the body, her treatment ranges from disgust to delight with the flesh (Kinnahan 56).

In most of her early poetry, Loy analyzes the female self as she sees its universal situation mirrored in her own life and in the life of her contemporaries (Kouidis 26). The feminist debates of her time seem to have stimulated her thinking about the poetic use of the female experience.

Few of the other female poets of the era spoke so honestly about the quotidian life of women. Also, Loy considered that it was her special talent as a poet to find poetry where it had not always been found before, that is, in the mundane and the fleshy, even in the excremental (Tuma 188).

This essay aims to analyze the representation of mothers and children in two poems by Mina Loy, "Parturition," and the subsection "Ada Gives Birth to Ova" of the long poem "Anglo-Mongrels and the Rose." I have always been fascinated by these two portraits of women giving birth. On the one hand, I am attracted by some of Loy's thematic and formal innovations in the poem "Parturition" such as its subject matter, its visual aspects, the use of simultaneity and juxtaposition as composition principles, and the vocabulary chosen to explore the dynamic creativity of a parturient woman, as well as to recreate the maternal body. "Ada Gives Birth to Ova" starts with a woman giving birth, but it differs completely in tone and vocabulary from "Parturition." The transgressive element lies on the sarcastic point of view, unorthodox language, and syntax chosen to depict the birth. There is neither tenderness nor complicity with a reader that cannot help laughing but, who, at the same time, feels somewhat uneasy. In "Parturition," the persona of the poem is a woman giving birth and in "Ada Gives Birth to Ova," the birth of Ova is narrated in a quite unsentimental tone, which suggests a modernist disillusionment with the family and with maternity. Loy resists the idealization of maternity and questions the figure of her own mother.

"Parturition," published in *Trend* in 1914, was the first poem ever written about the physical experience of giving birth from the parturient woman's point of view, detailing an area of femaleness rarely thought suitable for literature. Virginia Kouidis was the first critic to observe this, emphasizing the significance of this poem in the history of modern poetry as well as in the literature of modern sexuality (40). Carolyn Burke, biographer of Mina Loy, points out that fifty years before such a subject became acceptable, Loy traced what she called the "spatial contours" of childbirth in this poem (1985: 52). For Linda A. Kinnahan, "Parturition" depicts the intensely physical experience of labor through an unprecedented attention to the woman's body during childbirth (56).

The first stanzas emphasize the woman's physical pain and her alienation from the natural world. Pain is at the centre of the self and it breaks that nucleus of being by expanding in all directions: "I am the centre/ Of a circle of pain/ Exceeding its boundaries in every direction"

(Loy 1996: 4). The woman's feeling of isolation ("The business of the bland sun/ Has no affair with me," Loy 1996: 4) relegates everything but the dynamics of labor to a second level. In the third stanza, Loy tries to simulate with a compact and compressed free line the rhythmic contractions and expansions of labor (Burke 1985: 53):

Locate an irritation without
It is within
Within
It is without
The sensitized area
Is identical with the extensity
Of intension (Loy 1996: 4)

But this visual aspect of the poem does not only work at a formal level, but also at a psychological one. The self exists within an indifferent cosmos and the only way to achieve self-realization is vision. For Loy, women have been denied the vision of their own physical realities (Kouidis 32), so, by offering a different perspective of the maternal body during labor, Loy is trying to achieve the goal of a completely new definition of the female self, confirmed by the fact that the opening declaration "I am" reappears six times in the whole poem. Childbirth provides the means for self-comprehension and emphasizes the separateness between male and female experiences. Loy articulates male alienation from this extraordinary moment through simultaneity and juxtaposition. In the sixth stanza, the author contrasts the man's careless sexual freedom, "A fashionable portrait-painter/ Running up-stairs to a woman's apartment/ Sings" (Loy 1996: 5), with the difficult physical and spiritual situation of the parturient woman, depicted in the seventh stanza, whose body and mind are also following an upward movement, that of a contraction:

I am climbing a distorted mountain of agony
Incidentally with the exhaustion of control
I reach the summit
And gradually subside into anticipation of
Repose
Which never comes (Loy 1996: 5)

The stanza ends with an affirmation of the woman's active role and a suggestion of the special self-knowledge she is acquiring in this particular situation: "For another mountain is growing up/ Which goaded by the unavoidable/ I must traverse/ Traversing myself" (Loy 1996: 5).

The inanity of this painter's voice singing of female charm ("All the girls are tid'ly did'ly/ All the girls are nice," Loy 1996: 5) shows up, by ironic juxtaposition with the laboring voice of the female subject-in-question, the inaccuracy of conventional portraits of women, whether they be verbal or visual. The author displays a sense of outrage at the prevailing image of women as fragile beings and her critique of the sexual standards and social customs of her culture of origin are expressed in her satirically objective description of the fashionable artist (Januzzi 423).

The following stanzas juxtapose thoughts and physical sensations. As Carolyn Burke suggests, the woman is trying to think through the body and write from within its spatial contours (42). Her consciousness alternates analytical passages with vivid, concrete images. The horizon of pain is interrupted by the presence of a pleasure in childbirth suggested by some intensely erotic expressions such as "the foam on the stretched muscles of a mouth" (Loy 1996: 5), "a climax in sensibility" (Loy 1996: 5), and a "lascivious revelation" (Loy 1996: 6). These expressions reveal the importance the woman gives to all the bodily sensations she is experiencing in this unique moment. Loy resists the idealization of the moment of birth and, in a quite innovative way, focuses on what the mother feels through her skin and tissue.

After mountains of agony comes relaxation in the next stanza. The woman connects herself with the natural cosmos which had been alien to her body and feels part of "cosmic reproductivity" (Loy 1996: 7). At the same time, the speaker recognises the animal element in her "infinite Maternity" (Loy 1996: 7):

> For consciousness in crises   races
> Through the subliminal deposits of evolutionary processes
> Have I not
> Somewhere
> Scrutinized
> A dead white feathered moth
> Laying eggs? (Loy 1996: 6)

The baby is felt through its touch and its movements resemble those of a little animal: "Against my thigh/ Touch of infinitesimal motion/ Scarcely perceptible/ Undulation/ Warmth moisture" (Loy 1996: 7). The aesthetic and philosophic keys of these stanzas lie on the juxtaposition of abstract concepts about maternity and of the physical sensations of the process of becoming a mother. The woman experiences a new sense of belonging to the universe which has its roots in the psychological and in the physical. The parturient woman feels part of "evolutionary processes" (Loy 1996: 6) that lead her "Into the essence/ Of unpredicted Maternity" (Loy 1996: 6) and of a maternal continuum: "I am absorbed/ Into/ The was-is-ever-shall-be/ Of cosmic reproductivity" (Loy 1996: 7).

The speaker, by identifying herself with a cat, evokes again the purely physical elements of maternity which equal her to the rest of living beings:

Rises from the subconscious
Impression of a cat
With blind kittens
Among her legs
Same undulating life-stir
I am that cat (Loy 1996: 7)

Images from the insect world complete the previous ones and provide the speaker with a special knowledge of the world and of herself:

And through the insects
Waves that same undulation of living
Death
Life
I am knowing
All about
    Unfolding (Loy 1996: 7)

The final stanzas offer an ironic contrast with the rest of the poem. The intense physical and psychological experience of childbirth gives way to a cynical vision of mothers and women. The strong "I am" of the past stanzas has turned into "Each woman-of-the-people" (Loy 1996: 7). The image of female solicitude and the sisterhood of suffering suggest human affection among women, but imply the relative unimportance of those efforts (Kouidis 46): "Each woman-of-the-people/ Tip-toeing the red pile of the carpet/ Doing hushed service" (Loy 1996: 7). The "infinite Maternity" (Loy 1996: 6) and the "cosmic reproductivity" (Loy 1996: 7) have become "A ludicrous little halo"/ Of which she is sublimely unaware" (Loy 1996: 7). Suddenly, giving birth is not a source of self-knowledge, creativity and connection with the universe, but a conventional condition shared by many women who ignore their own creative potential. The poem ends with three irreverent lines which articulate the author's sarcastic vision of religion and add an unsentimental touch very typical of Loy: "I once heard in a church/ Man and woman God made them/ Thank God." (Loy 1996: 8). Loy seems to be attacking Christianity's idelogy of gender and the image of the master (male) creator. Marisa Januzzi emphasizes the ambiguity of these last lines, particularly the word "them," which may refer to man and woman or more specifically to sexual difference which God made. "Them" may also refer to babies, which in churches are said to have been made by God (426). The irony of the final line "Thank God" derives from the juxtaposition of the typical religious reading of the meaning of birth with the maternal poem written by Loy.

The poem "Anglo-Mongrels and the Rose" was written in Paris between 1923 and 1925. The first two instalments of the poem came out in the "Exile" issue (1923) of *The Little Review*, and the third in Robert McAlmon's *Contact Collection of Contemporary Verse* (1925). The poem was not published whole until 1982 in the volume *The Last Lunar Baedeker*, edited by Roger L. Conover. "Anglo-Mongrels and the Rose" is among the oddest of modernist long poems, a strange combination of satire, didactic commentary and lyrical mysticism. Though Loy was forty years old when she wrote the poem, it is an allegorical, parodic, and pseudo-narrative of the poet's ancestry, birth, and childhood (Perloff 134). We can say then that this is autobiography or automythology, and rather curious in its selection of autobiographical events. The reader needs some extra-textual biographical information about Mina Loy, otherwise he/she will have difficulties in understanding some sections which introduce characters who are not especially integrated into this cryptic personal mythology.

The poem has three sections of different length. The first one, "Exodus," focuses on Loy's father, Sigmund Löwy, a Hungarian jew who emigrated to London at the end of the XIX century. In "English Rose," Loy writes about her mother, Julia Bryan, who is called both Ada and Alice. The third section, "Mongrel Rose," is devoted to Ova, daughter of Exodus and Ada. Ova is a representation of Mina Loy as a child, a kind of ironic and sceptic version of herself. Her coming to this world anticipates her unconventional existence and is recreated in the subsection "Ada Gives Birth to Ova." Ada's pain is not comparable to the one felt by the woman in "Parturition" where pain appears as a natural consequence of the labor process and intensifies the parturient woman's consciousness of herself and the world. In contrast, Loy suggests that Ada's pain is grotesque because she cannot control it as she has done with her own body all her life. Ada does not seem to cooperate in this crucial moment, on the contrary, Loy emphasizes that the baby is extracted from her:

Her face
screwed   to the mimic-salacious
grotesquerie of a pain
larger than her intellect
  They pull
A clotty bulk of bifurcate fat
out of her loins
to lie
for a period while performing hands
pour lactoid liquids through
and then mop up beneath it
their golden residue (Loy 1985: 130)

It is difficult to find a more unsentimental description of the birth of a human being and a stronger sense of alienation between mother and child. The newborn is described not as a beautiful baby, but as "A clotty bulk of bifurcate fat" (Loy 1985: 130). Instead of being held by her mother, Ova is aseptically manipulated by "performing hands." If in "Parturition" the parturient woman is the protagonist, here the mother is absent and alien. Loy insists on Ova's exceptionality when describing her as "A breathing baby/ mystero-chemico Nemesis/ of obscure attractions" (Loy 1985: 131) and mentioning her "isolate consciousness" (Loy 1985: 131). Ova receives a mixed heritage from her Hungarian Jewish father and her English Protestant mother, but this mongrel condition is not seen as something positive by Ada. From her "ominous pillow," (Loy 1985: 132) Ova seems to remind her mother that she carries the genes of those who killed Christ:

So is the mystic absolute
the rose
that grows
from the red flowing
from the flank of Christ
thorned with the computations
of the old
Jehova's gender
Where Jesus of Nazareth
becomes one-piece

with Judas Iscariot
in this composite
Anglo-Israelite (Loy 1985: 132)

Ova is an Anglo-Israelite mixture of Jesus of Nazareth and Judas Iscariot, but blessed with a Jewish intellect. The last two stanzas insist on Ova's singularity and suggest her intelligence and independence despite a hostile family atmosphere where her mother remains distant. Her mongrel heart and smart eyes cast a determined spirit among clumsy maternal caresses:

Out of a fatted frown
this spirit pokes its eyes
its star tipped handy-pandies
darting on the air

Solemn and unsurprised
and clumsily
lapped by insensitive maternity
it lies
waving its brand new feet
and feeds
its mongrel heart on Benger's food
for infants (Loy 1985: 132)

In "Parturition," Mina Loy criticizes conventional notions of the individual and of aesthetic representation. A new mode of female consciousness breaks out of the confinement to which convention had relegated it. Loy represents the woman as an active subject in this crucial moment. Childbirth becomes the means for self-comprehension and releases the woman from dependence upon the male. By giving birth to the child, she also gives birth to the poem and to herself in an acknowledgement of female creative potential. Labor is not considered a means to an end, but as the unique work of the creative individual. As Virginia Kouidis points out, Loy rediscovers woman's limitation and helplessness and also woman's strength. She has proved the futurists' accusation of female animality, but has defied animality by using suffering creatively (46). The subsection "Ada Gives Birth to Ova" from the long poem "Anglo-Mongrels and the Rose" shows a certain disillusionment about childbirth and maternity. Loy recreates in a sarcastic and sometimes cruel way her mother's attitude towards her own birth. Julia, Loy's mother, is renamed Ada and Mina Loy herself becomes Ova. Loy criticizes Ada's aloofness in the process of giving birth and considers it a consequence of Ada's rejection of everything connected to the body. Whereas the woman in "Parturition" articulates the pain of contractions in a vivid way and experiences an intense physical closeness to her child, Ada's attempt to control her pain becomes grotesque and provokes a separation between mother and child. This poem is far from the tender animality suggested by "Parturition." Ada feels a certain disgust towards her daughter's physical aspect because it reminds her of her Jewish husband. She seems to have interiorized all the stereotypes of her time about Jews and, for her, Ova's mongrel condition is not a happy fact. Loy juxtaposes words from different categories of diction: the biological and psychological, the bestial and romantic, the educated and the vulgar, the scientific and the colloquial. The result is two poems that were transgressive in Loy's time and continue puzzling readers nowadays.

WORKS CITED

Benstock, Shari. *Women of the Left Bank: Paris, 1900-1940*. Austin: University of Texas Press, 1988.

Burke, Carolyn. "The New Poetry and the New Woman: Mina Loy." *Coming to Light: American Women Poets in the Twentieth Century*. Diane Wood Middlebrook, and Marilyn Yalom, eds. Ann Arbor: The University of Michigan Press, 1985. 37-57.

——. *Becoming Modern: The Life of Mina Loy*. Berkeley: University of California Press, 1997.

Januzzi, Marisa. "Mongrel Rose: The 'Unerring Esperanto' of Loy's Poetry." *Mina Loy: Woman and Poet*. Maeera Shreiber, and Keith Tuma eds. Orono: The National Poetry Foundation, 1998. 403-41.

Kinnahan, Linda A. *Poetics of the Feminine: Authority and Literary Tradition in William Carlos Williams, Mina Loy, Denise Levertov, and Kathleen Fraser*. Cambridge: Cambridge University Press, 1994.

Kouidis, Virginia M. *Mina Loy: American Modernist Poet*. Baton Rouge: Louisiana State University Press, 1980.

Loy, Mina. *The Last Lunar Baedeker*. 1982. Manchester: Carcanet, 1985.

——. *The Lost Lunar Baedeker: Poems of Mina Loy*. New York: Farrar, Straus and Giroux, 1996.

Ress, Lisa. "From Futurism to Feminism: The Poetry of Mina Loy." *Gender, Culture, and the Arts: Women, the Arts, and Society*. Ronald Dotterer, and Susan Bowers, eds. Selinsgrove: Susquehanna University Press, 1993. 115-27.

Tuma, Keith. "Mina Loy's 'Anglo-Mongrels and the Rose.'" *Mina Loy: Woman and Poet*. Maeera Shreiber, and Keith Tuma, eds. Orono: The National Poetry Foundation, 1998. 181-204.

Conrad's Entrapment into Imperial Ideology

HEM SHARMA PAUDEL

JOSEPH Conrad, in relation to imperialism, has received both positive and negative criticisms from different critics; early critics like Arnold Kettle appreciated him for his bold exposition of "the most horrifying [...] effects of imperialism," (63) whereas later postcolonial critics like Chinua Achebe have severely criticized him (while passing remark on Heart of Darkness) for constructing the image of Africa as barbaric and uncivilized and reducing the people to the members of a herd: "*Heart of Darkness* projects the image of Africa as 'the other world,' the antithesis of Europe and therefore of civilization, a place where man's vaunted intelligence and refinement are finally mocked by triumphant bestiality" (173). But the fact is that it is difficult and also impracticable to starkly place every writer into colonial or postcolonial; imperialist or anti-imperialist block, as Elleke Boehmer states of the colonial writers critical of colonial mission: "they partook of its values and symbolic language as well as of its privilege [...]. They intended to believe for instance that any impetus for change in the colony should, when it was necessary, come from the center, from Britain" (144). So, Conrad is consciously anti-imperialist and unconsciously imperialist because of his own entrapment into the ideological imperative of his day. A closer observation of his enormously complex novel *Nostromo* clearly reveals this idea.

Conrad was anti-imperialist and imperialist—anti-imperialist in his fearless exposition of the corruption of overseas domination and imperialist in his deep-seated mistrust of the natives and native political movements. On the one hand, he saw futility and illusion in imperialist philanthropy; on the other, he saw native people and society as primitive and degenerate. Thus, Conrad criticized imperialism while sharing many of its attitudes.

Conrad's Anti-imperialist Attitude in *Nostromo*

The conquest of the earth, which mostly means the taking it away from those who have a different complexion or slightly flatter noses than ourselves, is not a pretty thing when you look into it too much. What redeems it is the idea only. An idea at the back of it; not a sentimental pretence but an idea; and unselfish belief in the idea—something you can set up, and bow [...] down before, and offer a sacrifice to [...]. (*Heart of Darkness* 255)

Conrad had an unflinching respect for the facts of the world he lived in. The facts he found were not merely the glamour, adventure, colour and romance, but there is an uglier word as well: imperialism. Though Conrad does not use the word 'imperialism' as it was not a common vocabulary during his time, the growth of imperialism and the domination of countries from Africa, Asia and South America by Western powers was a very obvious reality of his time. Conrad's reading of imperialism was very much honest. He saw it corrupting the moral and rational judgment of the imperialists and turning them from idealist into cold mechanical beings governed only by the money-hunger. Besides this, the most significant fact about his writing is his exposition of the hypocrisy lurking behind the imperialist slogans of philanthropy.

Neither imperialism nor colonialism was (is) a simple act of accumulation and acquisition. They were supported and backed by impressive ideas: idea of peace, prosperity and progress; technological and scientific development; idea of bringing light and civilization, and that of introducing democracy and rule of law which was thought to be absent in the non-European world of barbarism and lawlessness.

Many writers supported these rationalizations and bright ideas whereas Conrad found them but to be sham. Conrad, in *Nostromo*, also demystified the American ideas of altruism and specialness, and its claim of righter of wrongs. He exposed how the 'business of empire,' once an adventure and often individualistic enterprise, had become the empire of business.

The novel is an analysis of the issues and conflicts which have dominated Third World countries. It examines the attempt to graft Western capitalistic enterprise, cultural norms, and political institutions, upon the stock of a peasant, economically underdeveloped country, recently emerging out of Spanish colonial rule. And the central metaphor, the bond and main source of the political, economic and cultural conflicts in Costaguana is, of course, the silver, which Conrad describes as the pivot of the moral and material events, affecting the lives of everyone in the tale. The exploitation of the silver which is "the symbol of the supreme importance of material interests" (219) from the province of Sulaco, by these foreigners like Gould and Holroyd very clearly refers to imperialism or new imperialism. Conrad has frankly spoken of this "great Contaguana undertaking" as "to put money into the pockets of Englishmen, Frenchmen, Americans, Germans and God knows who else" (197) to indicate the economic exploitation of Cataguana through the pervasive network of Europeans and Americans.

Objectively it is clear that the phrase 'material interests' stands for imperialism. The whole process and consequences of imperialist exploitation and Conrad's attitude towards it is so richly and concretely illuminated and reflected in the characterizations of Charles Gould and his American backer, Holroyd. It is also reflected in the strategy of bringing other characters like Mrs. Gould, Dr. Monygham and Decoud against the force of imperialism.

Gould's American backer, Holroyd, is portrayed as an imperialist dominated by money hunger, with an admixture of the white man's burden missionary zeal characteristic of the period to spread "purer form of Christianity" (Conrad 78). Holroyd is the very type of the Protestant ethic and the spirit of capitalism. He wants to spread Protestantism in Catholic countries and with it the culture and politics favourable to economic expansion. Holroyd's dream of introducing purer form of Christianity turns into nothing more than idolatry, as he looks upon his own God as a sort of influential partner, who gets share of profit in the endowment of churches. For this millionaire, Catholicism is a religion of "wood and tinsel" (Conrad 70), but his own religion transforms into the "religion of iron and silver" (Conrad 71). His idea of introducing justice, industry, peace or democracy becomes simply the means of creating favorable atmosphere for economic expansion.

All his lofty ideas are merely the cover-up or the mask for all-round invasion of Sulaco, or by indication whole of the South American continent. Despite the popularity of Anglo-Saxon racist political theories during this period which backed the United States as a natural alley of England, Conrad was hostile to the growth of United States power and its claim of moral right to run the world. In these lines Holroyd reveals his true mission:

> Now, what is Costaguana ? It is the bottomless pit of ten-percent loans and other fool investments. European capital had been flung into it with both hands for years. Not ours, though. We in this country know just about enough to keep indoors when it rains. We can sit and watch. Of course, someday we shall step in. We are bound to. But there is

> no hurry. Time itself has got to wait on the greatest country in the whole of God's universe. We shall be giving the word for every thing: industry, trade, law, journalism, art, politics, and religion from Cape Horn clear over to Smith's Sound, and beyond, too if anything worth taking hold of turns up at the North Pole. And then we shall have the leisure to take in hand the outlying islands and continents of the earth. We shall run the world's business whether the world likes it or not. The world can't help it—and neither can we, I guess. (Conrad 75)

Conrad's exposure of American moralistic and providential rationalisation of imperialism, in these lines, takes the form of a satire of the American financier Holroyd's missionary Christianity. Given Conrad's political judgment of the United States, Holroyd's prophecy of its dominance not only over Latin America but all over the world and not only economically but culturally has the sound of a triumphs of doom. Conrad perceives this ascendancy of material interests as a form of conquest. It is a concrete representation of American expansionism in Holroyd's prophecy. Charles Gould's faith is parodied by him, whose interest in furthering a pure from of Christianity, and whose faith in the manifest destiny of the United States cannot without irony be said to give ideal significance to his love of power. Conrad found in him the temperament of a puritan and "an insatiable imagination of conquest" (Conrad 75). Thus his slogan of purer form of Christianity or the greatest country in the whole of God's universe (in its connotation to altruism) are simply the means to spread the culture and politics favourable to (its) economic exploitation and economic expansion.

Thus, Conrad reveals, all those lofty ideals behind imperialism are sham and illusive, the real drive is the economic hunger of becoming rich by exploiting poor countries. This idea becomes as obvious as the daylight sun in the transformation of Holroyd's ideals and in his obscene blend of the religion with the materialist idioms.

A similar pattern appears in the character of Charles Gould in the process of his transformation from an ideal hero into a corrupt and soulless materialist. Gould is an idealist and like Kurtz he represents himself as an emissary of light in a land of darkness. And initially he wants to make the silver mine simply a "means not as an end" to bring "law, good faith, order, and security" (Conrad 74). But later the mine becomes an end in itself. The mine turns into a fetish and his high and elevated ideas grow into a part of "English talent of mere idealizing tendency in which no Englishman can exist without making a common fact a part of a fairy tale" (Conrad 184).

Slowly when he becomes obsessed with the material desire and the safety of the mine it becomes self-destructive, as this obsession to the mine makes him mad and insane with only the physical safety of the mine in his mind. The ideal of rational justice ceases to exist in the slow process of the identification of himself and his own safety with that of the mine. His passion for the mine has grown really irksome; it has become more intensive than anyone's passion for poetry, love or revenge. So, the passion now does not remain merely a passion, but changes into obsession. And the practical effect of emerging madness is to make Gould increasingly concerned with the physical safety of the Concession. From an ideal conception of political order which was to be implemented through the mine, Gould's vision gradually contracts to an obsession with the safety of the mine itself. The ideal of rational justice ceases to exist "on its only real or immaterial side" and becomes identified with the material agency through which it was to be realized (72). No longer the means to an end, the mine becomes the end itself, whose preservation and well-being are, in Gould's eyes, equivalent to the successful achievement of his dream. Gould Concession has insidiously corrupted his judgment by making him sick of bribing and intriguing merely to have his work left alone from day-to-day. Like his father he did not like to be robbed. And he identified himself with the mine and wanted to destroy it instead of surrendering:

> He was prepared, if need be, to blow up the whole San Tome mountain sky high out of the territory of the Republic. This resolution expressed the tenacity of his character, the remorse of that subtle conjugal infidelity through which his wife was no longer the sole mistress of his thoughts, something of his father's imaginative weakness, too, of the spirit of a buccaneer throwing a lighted match into the magazine rather than surrender his ship. (303-04)

This remarkable passage suggests not only the image of the conqueror, the alien who wishes to spoil the country rather than to take spoil from the country, but also the image of the anarchist who would rather bring everything down with him than accept partial or temporary defeat. Conrad's expressed view was that the capitalist is the greatest anarchist, and Gould's terrorism connects him with the subject of the anarchist tales. He becomes a terrorist when he reveals his preparation to blow up the mine, in rejecting Hirch's offer to sell him dynamite. The chief engineer of the railroad remarks that his policy is "radical [...] I mean going to the roots you know," and Gould replies, "why, yes [...] the Gould Concession has struck such deep-roots in this country, in this province, in that gorge of the mountains, that nothing but dynamite shall be allowed to dislodge it from there. It's my choice. It's my last card to play" (177). He wants to establish personal order over it, for good or bad. King of Sulaco, as he is called, is destroyed by his undertaking—his *Imperium in Imperio*. Freedom and independence which marks the earlier period of Charles Gould becomes alien now: "The mine had got hold of Charles Gould with a grip as deadly as ever it had laid upon his father" (331). Holroyd was well aware of this plan and perhaps it was suggested to Gould by Holroyd himself: "And that's how I've presented it to Holroyd" (177).

Gould being an anarchist and even a terrorist is suggested in a very remarkable and meaningful comparison between Charles Gould, the master of the mine and Hernandez the bandit, the master of the Campo:

> Has not the master of the mine any message to send to Hernandez, the mater of the Campo. The truth of the comparison struck Charles Gould heavily. In his determined purpose he held the mine and the indomitable bandit held the Campo by the same precarious tenure. They were equals before the lawlessness of the land. It was impossible to disentangle one's activity from its debasing contacts. (300)

This parallel between these two characters suggests how rash and irrational were the activities of Gould. As Hernandez was a bandit, involving in various demeaning activities of looting and killing, (threatening the travellers) the act of Mr. Gould was not less insidious to the people and the land. His debasing contact with Holroyd the imperialist and the capitalist had made him entirely an inhuman creature with only a single idea of the protection of the mine in his mind. He falls in the status of the bandit by threatening to destroy whole the land thereby endangering peace and prosperity of the land. He becomes not the 'saviour' or an emissary of light but an anarchist with his association with the sinister Holroyd.

Charles Gould is completely absorbed by matter, the 'material interests.' As the 'material interests' of the Concession increasingly come to dominate his attention, Gould sinks beneath the level of irrationality to a point at which all awareness seems to disappear in an almost total identification with the physical fact of the mine.

The gradual transformation of reason into madness marks the destruction of the feeling of independence and freedom which had characterized his early period of success. Under increasing pressure to ensure the safety of the Concession, Gould abandons his stance of a distanced manipulation of local politics and intervenes directly. Earlier he maintained a distance. He did not back one government over another:

> The extraordinary development of the mine had put a great power into his hands. To feel that prosperity always at the mercy of unintelligent greed had grown irksome to him [...]. It was dangerous. In the confidential communications passing between Charles Gould, the king of Sulaco, and the head of the silver and steel interests far away in California, the conviction was growing that any attempt made by men of education and integrity ought to be directly supported [...] the Ribierist party in Costaguana took a practical shape under the eye of the administrator of the San Tome mine. (127-28)

Thus Gould comes to feel that "There must be an end now of this silent reserve [...]. The material interests required form him the sacrifice of his aloofness" (415). The founding of the Occidental republic which is the eventual result of Gould's decision to give his direct support to Ribiera, represents consequently not the triumph of light but only another manifestation of the persistent tyranny which has always characterized Costaguana. This is the meaning of Dr. Monygham's prophecy:

> There is no peace and no rest in the development of material interests. They have their law, and their justice. But it is founded on expediency, and is inhuman; it is without rectitude, without the continuity and the force that can be found only in a moral principle, Mrs. Gould, the time approaches when all that the Gould Concession stands for shall weigh as heavily upon the people as the barbarism, cruelty, and misrule of a few years back. (419)

Thus the Occidental Republic established to restore peace and order, and to protect the wealthiest province from the misrule of the Interior falls under another trap of the tyranny of material interests. This very clearly suggests the invasion of external forces, that of imperialist Gould and Holroyd, in Costaguana that makes the local politics so unstable and liquid.

In *Nostromo*, the slow decay of idealism into irrationality is suggested not only in the allusions to the growing weight of the mine's autocracy or its increasing power to "crush innumerable lives in the expansion of its greatness (427-28) but is also implied in the references to the history of the financier Holroyd which is already dealt in this research. This decay and death of idealism into vulgar materialism that involves 'moral degradation of the idea' comes in a very powerful and touching manner when the narrator reports the profound and bitter feeling and experience of Mrs. Gould after 'incorrigible' Charles Gould falls victim to his own devotion to the mine mind and heart:

> She saw the San Tome Mountain hanging over the Campo, over the whole land, feared, hated, wealthy; more soulless than any tyrant, more pitiless and autocratic than the worst government [...]. He did not see it [...]. An immense desolation, the dread of her own continued life, descended upon the first lady of Sulaco. With a prophetic vision she saw herself surviving alone the degradation of her young ideal of life, of love, of work—all alone in the Treasure House of the world [...] she stammered out aimlessly the words: 'Material interest.' (427-28)

This recurring phrase, 'material interests' keeps so essential a part in the moral pattern of the book that its precise significance cannot be ignored. Objectively it is clear that it stands for imperialism. It is the whole process and consequences of imperialist exploitation, so richly, concretely and humanely illuminated throughout the length of the book. This quoted paragraph of the novel marks the climax of the novel which gives us the moral discovery of Mrs. Gould. Her moral discovery when she muttered the phrase 'material interests' reminds us the similar awakening in Kurtz in Conrad's novel, *Heart of Darkness* when he utters the very popular and often quoted phrase 'The horror! The horror!' But Charles Gould failed to know himself, his moral and political condition. This is the remarkable aspect that distinguishes him from his blood-brother, Kurtz. He could not acknowledge the horror in his corruption, dehumanisation and moral darkness.

In a nut shell, this destructive transformation of Charles Gould reveals that an imperialist like him or Holroyd the financier is not part of incarnation in an alien land. Imperial ideological bases that it brings civilization, law, order and prosperity to an uncivilized and degenerate world is but an illusion and trap. That is reflected in the gradual emergence of 'material interests' that leaves Charles Gould imprisoned in his own creation. Gould's San Tome mine becomes a tomb, a tomb in which he remains as fixed and immobile as a corpse.

This is how Conrad presented such imperialists not as emissaries of light and civilization, but as harbingers of economic exploitation. And their so-called civilizing plans and missions are merely an excuse for more corrupt and irrational practices. In addition to this, imperialism for Conrad was a trap. The material basis of imperialism does not provide a viable solution for non-Western backwardness, but instead breeds conflicts and unrest among the people.

Conrad's Imperialist Attitude in His Continuation of Imperial Ethos in *Nostromo*

> "Going up that river was like traveling back to the earliest beginnings of the world, when vegetation rioted on earth and the big trees were kings." (*Heart of Darkness* 275)

Conrad's imperialist position in *Nostromo* is not as explicit as it is in the above quoted lines from *Heart of Darkness*. It is not at the same time as explicit as his anti-imperialist attitude in the same novel, *Nostromo*.

Even if Conrad discerned irredeemable corruption in the imperial project of overseas domination, his representation of South American landscape, people and the politics is fashioned by the images and stereotypes founded by earlier pioneers of colonial discourses. What is it that makes Conrad a colonial or imperial author is his stereotypic representation of the South Americans as predominantly inferior and deceitful. So representation doesn't mean the photographic representation of South America; the act of representing the alien is saturated by political and ideological beliefs. Representation along with its close association with power serves as a legitimating source which functions as a standard to evaluate the objects of representation, namely, the society and its values. Since representation is always carried out from the position of power, it helps to fabricate truth about the alien people. So politics is involved in this act. The imperial ideology that Conrad perpetuates can be discerned in his representation of the landscape of South America, its people, its political movements and his emplotment itself.

The landscape of Costaguana, though not equally hostile as in *Heart of Darkness,* is indifferent to human activities. It transcends the Western attempt to rationalize and categorize it through the use of their common vocabularies and familiar idioms. It is incomprehensible and unfathomable in its vastness and mysteriousness. In the center of the landscape of *Nostromo* lies the darkness of the Golfo Placido. Like the night "without limit in space and time" (Conrad 220), it negates the form of creation and confounds the objects of everyday life into one homogenous obscurity: "sky, land, and sea disappear together out of the world when the Placido—as the saying is—goes to sleep under its black poncho" (Conrad 20). In the 'vastness' of the gulf "your ship floats unseen under your feet, her sails flutter invisible above your head" (Conrad 20). All things are "merged into the uniform texture of the night" (Conrad 245).

The darkness of the Golfo Placido not only transcends the physical structures of creation, it also transcends all levels of consciousness. When Decoud voyages into the Placido, he finds that "no intelligence could penetrate the darkness of the Placido Gulf" (Conrad 231) and that he was robbed of his power of analysis. He finds that his own emotional hold on the world, his love for Antonia, evaporate too and that he is reduced to a state of "a somnambulist" (Conrad 410).

And these stereotypic images of the South American region as incomprehensible, vast, dark and mysterious give evidence to its backwardness and its close affinity to barbaric nature. Thus, Conrad projected imperial viewpoint in his representation of Latin American landscape.

Conrad's representation of the people of Costaguana is equally offensive and caricatural. In general, the novel presents the Latin Americans as lazy, shiftless, thievish, criminal, primitive, uncivilized, barbarous and monstrous. Very few of the characters are natives and most often they appear in a violent and murderous mob, gang or the crowd.

When we contrast the image of the natives with that of the whites, the whites are rational, educated, practical, enterprising and in command of their own activities. Charles Gould is a technician trained in mining engineering. He is rational at the beginning (though irrational after he is corrupted by the mine) with idea of justice and order in his mind. Similarly Decoud is an intellectual and a poet. Mrs. Gould is a humanitarian, sympathy and generosity personified. But the natives are just the opposite. At the very general level the novel presents the Latin Americans as lazy, shiftless, and the likes, to which political order and economic progress must be brought from outside. The narrator observes the Indians and Negroes going to the San Tome mountain gorge as:

> The Indian boys leaned idly against the long line of little cradle-wagons standing empty; the screeners and ore-breakers squatted on their heels smoking long cigars; the great wooden shoots slanting over the edge of the tunnel plateau were silent; and only the ceaseless, violent rush of water in the open flumes could be heard, murmuring fiercely with the splash and rumble of revolving turbine-wheels [...]. (Conrad 93)

This short excerpt gives us a very classic picture of the Indian race as lazy, idle, empty-minded and silent. These qualities of the people become more pronounced as their 'picture' is contrasted with the 'ceaseless, violent rush of water' in the background. The native are "suffering and mute" (Conrad 83). Even this rhetoric of lazy native applies to the leader of the natives, Pedrito Montero:

> Pedrito, the younger, incorrigibly lazy and slovenly, had drifted aimlessly from one coast town to another, hanging about counting houses [...]. His ability to read did nothing for him but fill his head with absurd visions. His actions were usually determined by motives so improbable in themselves as to escape the penetration of a rational person. (Conrad 320)

Pedrito Montero is incorrigibly lazy and slovenly and his motives are irrational and impenetrable.

Conrad does not even refrain from eroticizing the natives along with their representation as savage. The narrator reminds us of the proselytizing mission of Father Corbelan among the wild Indians:

> Father Corbelan [...] had gone preaching to blood-thirsty savages, devoid of human compassion or worship of any kind [...]. He had baptized whole nations of Indians, living with them like a savage himself. It was related that the padre used to ride with his Indians for days, half-naked, carrying a bullock hide shield, and, no doubt, a long lance, too—who knows? That he had wandered clothed in skins, seeking proselytes somewhere near the snow line of the Cordillera. (Conrad 168)

These lines give us an exotic image of the Indians as half-naked and clothed in skins. This eroticizing tendency was one among many of the tenets of colonial writings.

These natives never appear as fully realized human beings, nor are they equal to rational and practical Europeans. Thus this representation of the Latin Americans as inferior and barbaric does nothing more than strengthen and reinforce the Western view of the non-Western people.

Next issue that places Conrad in imperial position is his political reflection and attitude proper. His representation of the overall politics of Costaguana is marked with 'Otherness.' Conrad's political attitudes are presupposed, and rhetorically reinforced by ethical markers: the Blancoes are good, the Monterists are evil.

For common readers or any contemporary American, the most compelling aspect of the work is Conrad's prescience: he forecasts the unstoppable unrest and 'misrule' of the Latin American republics, as Conrad puts it, quoting Bolivar, "governing them is like ploughing the sea" (161). Yet it would be incomplete to read Conrad's great work simply as an early prediction of what we see happening in twentieth century Latin America or any other Third World countries, with the strip of colonels, liberation forces, and American financed mercenaries. We need to see into the assumption of Conrad that all the native (Third World) liberation movements are corrupt and they can never stand independent of the Western influence.

Now, peasant movement of Hernandez, revolutions of Monteroes and Decoud's 'separatism' need to be addressed elaborately to evaluate Conrad's political reflections and his attitude. Latin America, for Conrad, is an unruly and unregenerate continent: "After one Montero there would be another, the lawlessness of a populace of all colours and races, barbarism, irremediable tyranny. As the great liberator Bolivar had said in the bitterness of his spirit, 'America is ungovernable. Those who worked for the independence have ploughed the sea'" (161).

Even the most ardent hater of imperialism and the most perceptive of the characters, Monygham and Decoud perceive the land as barbaric and unregenerate, let alone other characters like Charles and Holroyd. The narrator remarks that "the doctor did not believe in the reform of Costaguana" (307). As many critics have observed, Daphne Erdinast-Vulcan rightly perceives Decoud as "a sharer of Conrad's temperament and history" and as "a spokesman for the author" (New Casebooks 136). This author-figure's perception of the politics of the Republic of Costaguana elucidates Conrad's own view on the 'corrupt' and unregenerate politics of Latin America:

> Of his own country he used to say to his French associates: Imagine an atmosphere of *operá bouffe* in which all the comic business of

> stage statesmen, brigands, etc., etc., all their farcical stealing, intriguing, and stabbing is done in dead earnest. No man of ordinary intelligence can take part in the intrigues of *une farce macabre.* (134-35)

Thus Conrad represents Contaguana as a banana republic where all sorts of farcical stuffs are let loose. No one of the local politicians does have any serious intentions behind their slogans, except "stealing, intriguing and stabbing" (Conrad 162). Costaguana politics comes to the readers with full of "the cry of dark barbarism, the cloak of lawlessness, of crimes, of rapacity, of simple thieving" (Conrad 162).

This is the overall picture of the Latin American republic recently decolonized, yet fallen under the trap of both the imperialists and local farcical political games, as Conrad perceived it. But the central question is—has Conrad truly understood the local political trends and their independent history? Or are the history and politics of Costaguana externalized into 'Otherness' by his Anglo-vision?

Imperialism, as it is inhuman, unjust and exploitative, gave rise to resistant native cultures. It is historical fact that nationalism—restoration of community, assertion of identity, emergence of new cultural practices—as a mobilized political force advanced the struggle against Western domination everywhere in the non-European world. As imperialism increased in scope and in depth, so too, in the colonies (neo-colonies) themselves, the resistance was carried forward and they were informed by an actively provocative and challenging culture of resistance. This was a culture with a long tradition of integrity and power in its own right, not simply belated reactive response to Western imperialism.

To evaluate Conrad's attitude towards such anti-imperialist independence resistance movements, his perception and representation of Monterist revolution, peasant movement of Hernandez and separatist movement of the aristocratic Blancos have to be analyzed in a great detail. Monterist revolution is given a very negative colour and it is represented as bad mirror image of the populist nationalist cause of the Blancos represented by Decoud. Both the Monterists and Decoudeans speak for national honour and its freedom from foreign speculators. But the indigenous Monterist variety is given the status of a "riot" (Conrad 27) or a mob activity and the people involved in it as "*ladrones* and *matreros,* thieves and murderers from the whole province" (Conrad 24). And these "scoundrels and *leperoes*, who did not know the meaning of the word liberty," Girgio Viola says, "were not a people striving for justice but thieves" (Conrad 30). This comment from Gergio Viola, whom Conrad presents as a true follower and apostle of "liberty and Garibaldi" (Conrad 27), very clearly elucidates Conrad's presupposition about the natives that they don't deserve independence and freedom; it is only for the Europeans. The narrator remarks of the Viola: "And everywhere he had seen English men in the front rank of the army of freedom" (Conrad 38). These freedom fighters merely become the artificers of arson and destruction: "all the harm the mob managed to achieve was to set fire to one—only one—stack of railway-sleepers" (Conrad 26).

Conrad equally degraded these local people involving in this movement, as Pedrito Montero is said to have begun his career collecting "a small band of outlaws" (Conrad 129). Their struggle was against the foreign encroachment, against the accomplice of this "vast colonization scheme" (Conrad 129) and against "the surrender of the lands and the slavery of the people" (Conrad 140). But Conrad rather vulgarized their probably good intention:

> The brothers were organizing an army, gathering malcontents, sending emissaries primed with patriotic lies to the people, and with promises of plunder to the wild *Ilaneros*. Even a Monterist press had come into existence, speaking oracularly of the secret promises of support given by 'our great sister Republic of the North' against the sinister land-grabbing designs of the European powers, cursing in every issue 'miserable Ribiera,' who had plotted to deliver his country, bound hand and foot, for a prey to foreign speculators. (Conrad 129)

These lines demonstrate some resonances of Decoud's bitter and more subtle perception of the exploitation of the land by those foreign speculators "who were breaking into the treasure-house" (Conrad 151). But there is very much elemental difference in that the Monteroes are shown to be criminal at heart, and their motives are shown to be the plunder. All their slogans are no more than 'patriotic lies.' Even Decoud can't see some genuine purpose behind the liberation movement of Monteroes. He reads this revolution simply as the product of the dissatisfaction of Montero for not getting proper "share of this famous loan for national development" (Conrad 158); for not getting bribe and monetary gain out of the scheme of selling national honour to the foreigners. Decoud complains: "why didn't the stupid Sta Marta people give him a mission on to Europe, or something? He would have taken five years' salary in advance, and gone on loafing in Paris, this stupid, ferocious *indio*!'" (Conrad 158).

This is how these local leaders are seen; they never come into life as a rational and respectable human beings. The phrases like 'stupid, ferocious *indio,*' 'boastful indio,' 'stupid barbarian' or the likes recur time and again in the entire book.

There is a further excerpt that can clearly indicate, through his historian, Decoud, Conrad's perception of such movements. Decoud comments on the situation of Sulaco after the 'sudden outbreak' of the populace to his sister: "we had an awful riot—a sudden outbreak of the populace [...]. It's object, no doubt, was loot [...]" (Conrad 191). In this quoted piece, three words quite need our scrupulous attention: 'riot,' 'sudden,' and 'loot.' The independence movement of Costaguana is nothing more than a 'riot' or the rash mob activity. Second, there can't be any organized and independent history of the resistance. It's merely a 'sudden' outbreak without any substantial purpose and rational cause. Lastly it suggests that this protest is no political activity but simple act whose ultimate purpose is looting and thieving, killing and destroying, for their barbaric and 'semi-wild' nature permits such activities as very normal. Every Third World nation has its long, systematic and integrated history of the resistance; national liberation was (and is) its major and ultimate goal. Though some hints of such revolts in early periods are found and dealt with, but they have the same 'suddenness' and the people were "incited to revolt by the emissaries sent out from the capital, had risen upon their English chiefs and murdered them to a man" (Conrad 55).

Thus this overall picture of Conrad's representation of Costaguana politics reveals that his own political attitude was presupposed, that the natives were incapable of independence and unable to understand the refined political virtues like liberty and democracy.

Finally, Conrad's imperial stand-point is reflected in the overall coordinates of the plot, that all narrative enacts a passage from nature to culture. Indeed, as discussed earlier in the representation of landscape, the opening pages evoke the landscape of the gulf, a landscape without people, while the close celebrates the achieved society of the new republic. The narrator assures the readers that Sulaco after secession grows "rich swiftly," and experiences "a second youth, like a new life" (Conrad 413) and Captain Mitchel blankly assures the readers that a 'New Era' has dawned (Conrad 393) and that Decoud's vision of recession is "a glorious success" (Conrad 403). Robert Pen Warren also supports this idea. He claims: "We must admit that the society at the end of the book is preferable to that of the beginning" (50).

In addition to the emplotment and characterization that, on a closer observation, reveal the unconscious ideological biases of Conrad, we have to equally see his politics of exclusion and inclusion (or his politics of representation).

What is represented and how it is done is analyzed so far. The things represented are not the only possible stuff or material for the novelist. There is always the possibility of choice or selection. So, politics is involved in the act of representation; and what is left out remains equally important issue to address. Conrad does not give us what is outside the imperial world. All Conrad can see is a world totally dominated by the West, in which every opposition to the West only confirms the West's wicked power. In case of *Nostromo*, the world beyond the Cordillera (rest of the Costaguana) is rarely brought into the main narrative interest. Even if some events are reported, like the escape of Ribiera, as a passing comment, they directly or indirectly affect the smooth working of imperialist exploitation. There is only one man in the capital of the country worth talking, Morage, the consultant of the Gould Concession. Rest of the people except Europeans, their all sorts of affairs, for Conrad, are not worth representing. If any of them are represented and their activities reported, it is only because they are dangerous threat to the European authority. They are only the 'monstrous' and 'primitive' Monteroes, the 'bandit' Hernandez, and the demagogues Gamacho and Fuentes. Otherwise the entire land is blank and dark like 'Placid Culf'; there are only impenetrable jungles of the Campo, and tall mountain peaks like Higuerota.

Hence, Conrad's explicit denunciation and implicit propagation of imperial ideology has, to this point, made his ambivalent position crystal clear. But there is still one more issue to be analysed to reveal his position in between the imperialists and the imperialists.

Conrad's Ambivalence in His Treatment of the Issue of History

Next issue for analysis is the idea of 'history' as it appears in Conrad's *Nostromo*. Conrad's attitude is ambivalent in this case too. The view of 'history' popular in the heydays of Empire was that the history of man is a logically sequential progression beginning in the darkness and pointing towards the light. Similar attitude appears in Conrad's another novel, *Heart of Darkness.* For Marlow at the opening of the novel, the progress of the civilization has been marked by the steady conquest of the darkness by the idea, of emotion by reason. To Captain Mitchel, who is the spokesman in Nostromo for this 'historical' point of view, the career of the Gould Concession describes such an upward curve and he speaks confidentially in the closing chapter of the great future of the separatist movement which has saved the San Tome mine "intact for civilization for a great future" (397). It is this assumption of progress and of fulfilment of Gould's ambition to turn the power of the mine to the service of the idea, which determines the form of Captain Mitchel's long narrative in the last chapters of the novel. Mitchel accepts the chronological order of history, speaks of the statue of Charles as an "anachronism" (396), and follows, the natural order of events because this linear progression expresses to him the reality of the historical process. The structure of Mitchel's narrative reflects the assumption of all those who accept the validity and success of the humanizing work of civilization and who see history as the record of this irreversible process.

This is the 'stereotyped' version of history which regards that only the European presence marks the beginning of true history, as Sir John thinks that the introduction of his railway marks the beginning of Costaguana history: "Has anything ever happened here for a hundred years before today?" (42). But Conrad does not leave this concept of history unquestioned. The narrator, who frames the story of Gould, sees that Mitchel's sense of historical progress is an illusion. It appears first in the narrator's remark that "Captain Mitchel had not much penetration of any kind" (282). Mitchel speaks high of the characters like don Juste Lopez, as "actual chief of the state" and a "first-rate intellect" (1393), the famous Hernandez as "Minister of War" (394) and Nostromo as "the popular hero of the revolution" (396). But the reader, of course, is well aware of the shady past of Lopez, who has been all prepared to surrender Sulaco to the Monterist tyranny in order to keep up the pretence of parliamentary institutions, of Hernandez's banditry, and Nostromo's stealing of the treasure. Next, the most perceptive of the characters, Decoud sees Mitchel as an absurd "sound box":

> 'No, but just imagine our forefathers in morions and corselets drawn up outside this gate, and a band of adventures just landed from their ships in the harbour there. Thieves, of course. Speculator, too. Their expeditions, each one, were the speculations of grave and reverend persons in England. That is history, as that absurd sailor Mitchel is always saying.' (151)

So, Decoud regards those Europeans not as historians but as speculators and their sense of history simply speculations. The real movement of history for Conrad is not linear but cyclical. It traces not a rise from the darkness but repeats the pattern of Costaguana politics in which revolution breeds another revolution.

But when we try to bring this cyclical theory of history down to the earth, the causes of this regressive repetition have to be discerned. First cause Conrad suggested is the 'moral darkness' of the people and their barbaric nature as elaborated earlier. The narrator explains the cause of their recurrence of revolutions as: "This will appear less incredible by the reflection that the fundamental causes were the same as ever, rooted in the political immaturity of the people, in the indolence of the upper classes and the moral darkness of the lower" (321).

Thus the fundamental cause is the nature of the local people, either their political immaturity and their idleness or their immorality and irrationality. Thus this description fits in the imperial view that since the natives are immature and in the state of perpetual childhood, foreign rule, European (American) in particular, is essential.

The second fundamental cause is the all corrupting effects of the material interests or the idolization of it. Economic benefit becomes the all absorbing end. So, the imperialists and the rulers under their influence think of nothing more than their petty interests, the people and 'the workers' are left exploited at their worst condition. And this rise of the autocracy (of the new imperialism) breeds resentment among the marginalized and revolts and revolutions crop up in a violent rush. This is suggested in the transformation of Gould's idealism into "more soulless" and "autocratic" tyrant: "She saw the San tome mountain hanging over the Campo, over the whole land, [...] more soulless than any tyrant, more pitiless and autocratic than the worst government, ready to crush innumerable lives in the expansion of its greatness" (427-28). Therefore, this expansion of imperialist exploitation, suggested by the 'San Tome mountain,' becomes the main source of further revolutions and bloodshed.

Thus, Conrad's ambivalence in the dealing of the Costaguana history is very much clear; the political unrest is due to the moral darkness of the people and the extension of imperialist exploitation.

Conclusion

Now, after observing his both anti-imperial and imperial positions, it is beyond the shadow of a doubt that Conrad both criticized and reproduced the imperial ideology of his time. Conrad's limitation is that even though he could see clearly that on one hand imperialism was essentially pure dominance and land-grabbing, he could not then conclude that imperialism had to end so that natives could lead lives free from European domination. As a creature of his time, Conrad could not grant the natives their freedom, despite his severe critique of the imperialism. In this regard it is relevant to end this paper with Said's remark about the enslavement of the colonialist writers by the colonial ideology:

> Yet all these works, which are so indebted to Conrad's anti-imperialist irony [...] argue that the source of the world's significant action and life is in the West, whose representations seem at liberty to visit their fantasies and philanthropies upon a mind-deadened Third World. In this view, the outlying regions of the world have no life, history, or culture to speak of, no independence or integrity worth representing without the West. And when there is something to be described it is, following Conrad, unutterably corrupt, degenerate, irredeemable. (xxi)

Thus, though Conrad, in his novel *Nostromo*, is critical of colonialism, he implicitly retained the imperialist attitudes of the past.

WORKS CITED

Achebe, Chinua. "An Image of Africa: Conrad's *Heart of Darkness*." *The Story and Its Writer: An Introduction to Short Fiction.* Ed. Ann Charters. 4th ed. Vol. 2. Boston: Bedford, 1995. 1373-78. 2 vols.

Boehmer, Elleke. *Colonial and Postcolonial Literature.* New York: OUP, 1995.

Conrad, Joseph. *Heart of Darkness. Literature.* Ed. James H. Pickering and Jeffrey D. Hoeper. 3rd ed. Houndsmills: Macmillan, 1991. 252-309.

——. *Nostromo.* London: Penguin, 1994.

Kettle, Arnold. *An Introduction to the English Novel.* Vol. 2. New York: Hutchinson, 1953. 2 vols.

Said, Edward W. *Culture and Imperialism.* London: Vintage, 1993.

Warren, Robert Pen. "'The Great Mirage': Conrad and *Nostromo*." *Selected Essays.* New York: Random House, 1958.

❑❑❑

William Faulkner's *The Sound and the Fury* as a Portrayal of Abnormal Psychology

MALLIKARJUN PATIL

WILLIAM Faulkner was a great American novelist of the 20th century. He was a fine short story writer too. He is known for his intricate narrative technique. Faulkner has written works of fiction, which establish his vision of mankind, and they speak of man's dignity and social position. Faulkner got many prizes like National Book Award, twice Pulitzer Awards and the Nobel Prize for Literature in 1949.

William Faulkner was born in New Albany in 1897. His great grandfather had moved from Tennessee to Mississippi where he was a plantation owner, colonel in the Confederate Army, railroad builder, and author of a popular novel, *The White Rose of Memphis*. Faulkner's family moved from New Albany to Oxford in Mississippi when William was just five. William had his basic education there and then went to Canada and joined the Royal Air Force. On return, he became a postmaster. He made an effort to do education at University.

In the beginning Faulkner made an effort to write poetry. Phil Stone was his early mentor. Mr. Stone helped him publish his book of poems *The Marble Faun*. Later, Faulkner lived in New Orleans and befriended Sherwood Anderson. The latter encouraged him to write the novel *Soldier's Pay* (1926). Faulkner made a walking tour of Europe and wrote the novel *Mosquitoes*.

On return, Faulkner hit upon the idea of making Yoknapatawpha, a fictitious county for his later works. This town is based on his experience in the town of Lafayette, Oxford as its seat. He wrote *The Sound and the Fury* (1929), *As I Lay Dying* (1930), *These Thirteen* (1931) and *Absalom, Absalom* (1936). His collections of short stories include *Sanctuary* (1931), *Light in August* (1932), *Doctor Martino and Other Stories* (1934), *Pylon* (1935), *The Unvanquished* (1938) and *Go Down Moses* (1942). His *Knight's Gambit* (1949) is a book of detective stories.

Some of Faulkner's novels of the later period are *The Wild Palms* (1939), *The Hamlet* (1940) and *Intruder in the Dust* (1948). Faulkner also wrote a play called *Requiem for a Nun* (1951), while *A Fable* (1954) is an allegory. His last work was *The Receivers* (1962), a nostalgic comedy of boyhood.

William Faulkner's novel *The Sound and the Fury* has its title from Shakespeare's play, *Macbeth* and has similar kind of despairing life. The concerned passage in *Macbeth* is as follows:

> To-morrow, and to-morrow, and to-morrow,
> Creeps in this petty pace from day to day,
> To the last syllable of recorded time,
> And all our yesterdays have lighted fools
> The way to dusty death. Out, out, brief candle!
> Life's but a walking shadow, a poor player
> That struts and frets his hour upon the stage.
> And then is heard no more. It is a tale
> Told by an idiot, full of sound and fury
> Signifying nothing.

The novel *The Sound and the Fury* is about the declining kind of life of an American Southern family. This is about decline of life in modern times between the two World Wars. It is said, unlike Cooper, Hawthorne, Melville and Poe and later Henry James, Faulkner, Hemingway, Passos and Fitzgerald wrote of life realistically. Hemingway's *The Sun Also Rises* typifies the attitude of all these writers who are committed to the harsh realities of modern life. Faulkner shows us the decadent society haunted by ghosts of the past. The American fiction of the inter-war years is that of despair and pessimism. In form and style these novelists were experimental too. Faulkner that way belongs to the elite of Henry James James, Joyce, Joseph Conrad, Marcel Proust and others. William Faulkner as a distinguished novelist has tried to depict the predicament of man in modern times. It is said how Faulkner wrote the novel:

> "*The Sound and the Fury* is William Faulkner's favorite among his novels for he found it the most difficult, ambitious and challenging to write: 'I must judge it on the basis that one which caused me the most grief and anguish, as the mother loves the child who became the thief or murderer more than the one who became the priest.' In answer to a question asked by a group of students from Mississippi which of his novels he considered the best, Faulkner replies, '*The Sound and the*

Fury still continues to move me.' Obviously, it is the one that he feels the 'most tender toward,' the one into which he says 'I have written my guts.'"[1]

Faulkner describes his experience of the novel thus:

"I wrote it five separate times, trying to tell the story, to rid myself of the dream which would continue to anguish me until I did [...]. It began with a mental picture. I didn't realize at the time it was symbolical. The picture was of the muddy seat of a little girl's drawers in a pear tree, where she could see through a window where her grandmother's funeral was taking place [...]. I had already begun to tell the story through the eyes of the idiot child, since I felt that it would be more effective as told by someone capable of knowing what happened, but not why. I saw that I had not told the story that time. I tried to tell it again, the same story through the eyes of another brother. That was still not it. I tried to gather the pieces together and fill in the gaps by making myself the spokesman. It was still not complete,—not until fifteen years after the book was published, when I wrote as an appendix to another book the final effort to get the story told and off my mind, so that I myself could have some peace from it."[2]

The story of the novel is related to Caddy's loss of virginity as viewed by her three brothers, Benjamin (Benjy), Quentin and Jason. Each of them gives his own point of view. Faulkner shows extraordinary skill and virtuosity in getting the first three sections of the novel narrated by them. In section IV he takes the responsibility of filling the gap and rounding out the novel with a larger perspective. The genesis of the novel began as:

"That began as a short story; it was a story without a plot, of some children being sent away from the house during the grandmother's funeral. They were too young to be told what was going on and they saw things only incidentally to the childish games they were playing, which was the lugubrious matter of removing the corpse from the house [...] etc. And then the idea struck me to see how much more I could have got out of the idea of the blind self-centeredness of innocence, typified by children, if one of these children had been truly innocent, that is, an idiot. So the idiot was born and then I became interested in the relationship of the idiot to the world that he was in but would never be able to cope with and just where could he get the tenderness, the help, to shield him in his innocence."[3]

Faulkner's novel has a wonderful structure. As we know he was a great experimentalist. So he packs his novel not with events and incidents but with sense and nonsense. Actually very few events occur in the external world and they can be easily recounted as follows:

> "The grandmother dies in 1898. The girl Candace (Caddy) has an affair with Dalton Ames by whom she is made pregnant. She is married to Herbert Head in April 1910. However, the birth of her illegitimate child Miss Quentin (named after brother Quentin) causes the annulment of the marriage. Her brother Quentin, who is at Harvard, commits suicide in June 1910. Mr. Compson, the father of the children—Benjy, Quentin, Jason and Caddy—dies in 1912. Caddy's daughter, who has been living at the Compson house, elopes with a 'carnival man,' taking away with her the money that her uncle Jason had cheated her of. Subsequently Jason desperately tries to capture her but in vain. Even while this chase is going on the old Negro female servant of the Compsons attending the Easter Sunday service on 8 April 1928 is moved to ecstasy by a visiting preacher."

It is said the first three units form one unit of the story and the fourth one another. In the first three are recorded the impressions and reactions of the three brothers to certain incidents of the past and to what they are doing in the present. It is their private world that is revealed to us by the use of the stream of consciousness technique. The author is invisible in all this. Still each of the first three sections gives different impressions as different persons with different perspectives write them. For example, Benjy speaks just from sensations; Quentin, from an abstract mode; and Jason, from a kind of logic. Faulkner seems to tell us that truth cannot be easily got in life. Once he said, "There are thirteen ways of looking at a blackbird." Olga W. Vickery observes, "The theme of *Sound and the Fury*, as revealed by the structure, is the relation between the act and man's apprehension of the act, between the event and the interpretation [...]. Each man creates his own truth [...] truth is a matter of the heart's response as well as the mind's logic."[4] The novel makes use of interior monologue to reveal the personalities. The consciousness of Benjy, Quentin and Jason is well reflected in differing styles, images and syntax. The novel that way may be called a 'polyphonic composition.' Still each of the first three sections has some differences. For example, section I narrates the family story for the last thirty years. It gives clues for the next sections; section II gives special information about Quentin's joining

Harvard, Caddace's marriage and Quentin's suicide; and section III is about Jason's affairs after Caddy's disappearance, in section IV, details are about Quentin's elopement and Jason's bankruptcy.

The gist of the story may be as follows. The Compson family had once been a good one, but the current generation had done everything to ruin the name of Compson. In the little Mississippi city in which the Compsons lived all laughed and made slighting remarks when the name Compson was mentioned.

Mrs. Compson has come from a gentile family but she married Mr. Compson of the degenerated family. She regrets of this for the last eighteen years. Her first son Benjamin is her great problem as he is an idiot. The second son Quentin is a reckless fellow known for his vulgarity. The third child Caddace is known for her wayward behavior. She is the only person to quieten Benjy, as is known otherwise. She did not allow the other members of the family including the Negro workers to tease Benjy. She loved the other people too.

Quentin is moody and he loved Caddace. It is said he loved her not as a sister but as a woman and she returned his love for him. Caddace loved Mr. Ames and got pregnant. She loved Sydney Herbert Head and married him with the condition that he should provide a job for Jason, her last brother. Quentin did not like Caddace marry Herbert Head, the banker. He said she couldn't marry him as he (Quentin) had an incest relation with his sister. He is quite wild. At last Quentin, when he is doing education at Harvard, commits suicide. The occasion is Caddace's marriage to Herbert Head. Mrs. Compson reigns herself to one more cross.

For some unknown reason, Head does not entertain his wife after she delivers her first girl child Quentin, named after her late brother. The Compson family does not shelter her. But they shelter her daughter. Jason believes that Caddace, the girl is born to Quentin though the others do not believe it. Caddace stays away from the little town for many years.

Quentin is as wild as her mother. She is just like her mother in manners. Caddace sends money for Quentin regularly. But Mrs. Compson burns her checks for she does not want Caddace's ill-gotten money. Mr. Compson dies soon in 1912. Jason becomes the head of the family. He blames Herbert Head refused to accept Caddace, for she has borne an illegitimate child. He feels sad because Head did not get him a job.

Hating his sister, Jason gets checks from another bank and gives them to his mother for burning; while he forges her signature on the checks sent by Caddace and gets cash. He plays the money in market.

Quentin hates Jason as much as he does her. They quarrel often. Mrs. Compson supports the girl's case. Once a show team comes to the town and Quentin takes up with one of the performers. One night she elopes with him. She elopes even with Jason's three thousand dollars. Jason feels sad and lodges a complaint against her. He tries to catch her in vain. Yet the money she has stolen is of her mother's, which Jason has manipulated for himself. Jason feels cheated and he gets enraged. He believes that everyone laughs at him because of his horrible family—because Benjy is an idiot, Candace, a lost woman, Quentin a suicide, and the girl Quentin, a village harlot and a thief. He forgets that he too is a thief and has a mistress. He feels cursed. In a fit of rage he beats Benjamin. But he regains his composure and feels what the servant Dilsey says that she sees the beginning and end of life. The life of the family is at a sad end finally.

Critics feel that the novel is about abnormal psychology of the Southern family. It is about degeneration. It is too private, too mired in the psychic realm, and too inarticulate about social forces that are more clearly revealed in Faulkner's later works. The novel is about filth and vulgarity. According to Cheryl Lester, the novel is about the black suffering. However, the most important facts about the success of the novel are that it is moving rather than enlightening upon an incident or situation. It is observed that, "The novel's stunning technical innovations partially account for its success."[5]

REFERENCES

1. William Faulkner, Introduction, *The Sound and the Fury*, Introduction by P.P. Sharma. Bombay: CUP, 1995, 12.
2. *Ibid.*, 14.
3. *Ibid.*, 15.
4. Olga W. Vickery, *Ibid.*, 16.
5. Cheryl Lester, "Racial Awareness and Arrested Development: *The Sound and the Fury* and the Great Migration (1915-1928), *A Cambridge Companion to William Faulkner*, ed. Phillip M. Weinstein. Cambridge: CUP, 1995, 123.

❑❑❑

The Novels of Jean Rhys as Studies in Inverted *Odyssey*

CHAITALI GORAI

> "[…] as if you had always done that—lived in a few rooms and gone from one to the other. The light is different colour every hour and the shadows fall differently and make different patterns. You feel peaceful, but when you try to think it's as if you're face to face with a high dark wall […] and before you know where you are it is night […]." (*Voyage in the Dark*, 120)

PARALLELISM can be drawn between the Homeric epic *The Odyssey* and the novels of Jean Rhys, as their works are based on themes that are similar. The motif of journey in quest for home and the continuous battles for the sake of survival unite these works. Then in what respect can the novels of Rhys be termed as an inverted *Odyssey*? Similar yet different is the thematic treatment of Rhys from that of Homer. Though Rhys uses the same themes as Homer, she moulds it into a new pattern through her creative genius.

In *The Odyssey*, Odysseus, the king of Ithaca, responds to the call of Menelaus to avenge the dishonour of the Greeks and joins the team of warriors in the journey to Troy. While returning to Ithaca he encounters many adventures finding himself among the Cicones at Ismarus, the Lotophagi, and the Cyclops Polyphemus. His voyage is not only confined to the islands on the sea, but in Book XI he descends into Hell and discourses with the ghosts of the deceased heroes. Odysseus voyages from island to island, embarking on unknown shores, with the least knowledge of what lies in wait for him. Every adventure is a new enriching experience. In the novels of Rhys her protagonists engage themselves travelling from place to place, continually shifting, with hope for a better prospect. Each experience brings for them something new making them hopeful but finally leaving them frustrated. Unlike *The Odyssey*, which is a tale of adventures, the protagonists of Rhys make a gradual progress through their experience towards their destiny. For instance, in *Quartet* with Stephan's arrest Marya looks forward to the Heidlers for protection. Temporarily she feels secured: "How gentle he is [...]. All my life before I knew him was like being lost on a cold, dark night" (66). But she later realizes that her existence was like the fox in the zoo: "Up and down it ran, up and down, and Marya imagined that each time it turned it did so with a certain hopefulness as if it thought that escape was possible. Then, of course, there were the bars" (124). In *After Leaving Mr. Mackenzie*, Julia Martin arrives at London with the hope of being reunited with her family after being a discarded mistress of Mr. Mackenzie. But she is treated "as if she were something out of the zoo" (73). She feels herself 'old and forsaken' (77) being 'filled with melancholy terror' (77). So for the Rhysian characters it is a journey in both physical and psychological spheres. Marya shifts from room to room, hotel to hotel, person to person and Julia from Paris to London and being disillusioned once more returns to Paris. In *Voyage in the Dark*, Anna Morgan's sad journey from innocence to experience has been focused. Cheated by Walter, the man she trusted with her life, the grim reality of existence is revealed to her. She is doubly cheated. First by her stepmother Hester with whom she comes to England from West Indies and then by her lover. In her homeland she was always curious about England. "I had read about England ever since I would read [...]" (15) but when there she found things difficult: "It was as if a curtain had fallen, hiding everything I had ever known" (7). Here the colours smells and the feelings that one felt were entirely different. She couldn't get used to the cold and detested those gray streets. It was very depressing for her. Sasha Jansen in *Good Morning, Midnight* arrived at the end of her journey. Through her physical and psychological journey she discovers that "All rooms are the same [...] have four walls, a door, a window or two [...] a place where you hide from the wolves outside" (38). Psychologically she feels that shifting continuously from place to place has wiped off her identity, someone with "no pride, no name, no face, no country" (44) belonging nowhere: "like one of those straws which floats round the edge of a whirlpool and is gradually sucked into the center, the dead center, where everything is stagnant [...] calm [...]" (44). Antoinette in *Wide Sargasso Sea* comes to England with her husband from Jamaica. When in the island she travels from Coulibri Estate to the convent after their house is burnt, from the convent to the Windward Islands for honeymoon after her marriage and then again backs to the Jamaican islands. With her constant shift of places various facts are revealed to her—that her mother dislikes her, that her marriage has only been a treaty between her stepbrother and her husband. The final blow comes with the fact that her husband did not love her. This breaks her. Grace Poole, the woman in England who was appointed to look after her recollects her as a "girl who lives in her own darkness [...]" (142). So while the experiences of Odysseus are little laurels that only enhance his heroism, the characters of Rhys develop themselves through their experiences. They progress from one step to another through their experiences, which help them to arrive at a certain conclusion. The development of the plot is based on their experiences. Technically, one experience is linked with the other. But in *The Odyssey* there may not be any textual gap if one adventure of Odysseus is snapped off. The adventures are events with only one cord to link them together—that they happen in the life of a hero named Odysseus.

Odysseus sails off from the coast of Ithaca to help the Greeks in the war. He reaches Troy, destroys the army and returns to Ithaca victorious. On his way he endures various perils at sea. For instance his adventure at Laestrygonia with Antiphates in Book X, whereof twelve ships he lost eleven with all his men. Then he went to the Isle of Aea where half of his men were turned into swine by Circe. He stayed with Circe for a year in order to retrieve them. In spite of innumerable sea hazards like a hero he is ever victorious and finally reaches Ithaca. With his unification with Telemachus and Penelope all his efforts bear fruit. In the world in which the Rhysian characters live they have to continuously fight for survival. They are peered with the forces of the society, which are more powerful than themselves. They are poisoned and stabbed by the only weapon that can give them sustenance: love. Though they are repeatedly misused each time they "got up and staggered on, bleeding and muddy" (*Quartet* 96). Suicide is an easy solution for such a miserable life that they lead. But they do not give in, pursuing courageously "She [Rhys] recognized that beneath the passivity and self-destructiveness of women there was a willingness to engage in a desperate struggle for survival, just as beneath the surface ugliness of their lives there was a yearning for beauty, a new dress, an attractive room" (Staley 13). Elgin W. Mellown comments that "the women upon whom Rhys centers her attention is indeed always a victim" (Carr 4). The little sculptor tells Marya: "You're a victim [...]. Victims are necessary so that the strong may exercise their will and become more strong" (58) or as Julia Martin had realized: "It's always like that. When you are tottering, somebody peculiarly well qualified to do it comes along and shoves you down. And stamps on you" (49) or as Sasha in her mind says to Mr. Blank: "There must be the dark background to show up the bright colours. Some must cry so that the others may be able to laugh the more heartily" (29). Anna Morgan, after having been abused and abandoned in England dreams of a return to an island: "[…] the ship was sailing very close to an island, which was home except that the trees were all wrong. These were English trees, their leaves trailing in the water. I tried to catch hold of a branch and step ashore, but the deck of the ship expanded" (140). She knew that once caught there was to be no escape. Walter Allen sums up the character of Antoinette as "[…] a young woman […] who is hopelessly and helplessly at sea in her relations with men, a passive victim doomed to destruction" (Carr 4). Odysseus's battle ends with his arrival at Ithaca but Rhysian protagonists battle forever. They are caught in the dirty quick-sand of society in which they have to survive. They want to strike roots trying to have a firm hold but fail, they try to struggle to make escape possible but the more they struggle the deeper they sink. They sink suffocated leading a death-in-life existence.

Odysseus is the king of the small island of Ithaca. He led a happy homely life with his wife Penelope and son Telemachus. James I. Armstrong sums up *The Odyssey* as: "The return of Odysseus, the restoration of his kingdom and the reunion of Odysseus with his faithful wife Penelope and his young son Telemachus comprise the basic subject matter of the Odyssey" (Butcher and Lang vii). After the Trojan war Odysseus is anxious to return to Ithaca but did not know the passage. He has a sacred bond with the land and is not uprooted from it like the Rhysian protagonists. He is also attached to Penelope to whom he longs to return. For once he falters, doubtful that perhaps Penelope has forgotten him after all these years and has married one of the neighboring kings. In Book XI with his descent into hell he meets the spirit of his deceased mother. His anxiety to know of his relations is reflected in the volley of questions that he puts to his mother: "[…] necessity was on me to come down to the house of Hades to seek to the spirit of Theban Teiresias. For not yet have I drawn near to the Achaean shore, nor yet have I set foot on mine own country, but have been wandering evermore in affliction […] tell me of my father and my son […] of my wedded wife […] doth she abide with her son and keep all secure, or hath she already wedded the best of the Achaeans?" (Butcher and Lang 156-57). His mother replies that Penelope "with steadfast spirit in thy halls; and wearily for her the nights wane always and the days in shedding of tears. But the fair honour that is thine no man hath yet taken" (Butcher and Lang 157). She informs that his father "lies sorrowing and nurses his mighty grief, for long desire of thy return" (Butcher and Lang 157). Odysseus is touched and is filled with grief. On his return after much difficulty he receives a warm reception from his family and people. The protagonists of Rhys step out of their home but as soon as they take their first step their home ceases to exist. In many of her novels this home does not exist at all. The characters step out in search of it but never arrive. Their attempt proves nothing but futile Marya's father and mother had died. She had to earn to keep herself going. She had an aunt who did not have any consideration for her. Stephan had reflected, "they didn't seem to care in the least what became of her" (17). Dreaming to build a home she comes to Paris with Stephan leaving England and her relations behind. But even before her dream takes a complete shape Stephan is arrested for being a dealer in stolen objects of art. Feeling lost she readily accepts the company of the Heidlers. But she becomes a prey to the desire of Mr. Heidler. She longs for Stephan to return. With his return "an irrational feeling of security and happiness took possession of her [...]. It was extraordinary, but there it was. This was the only human being with whom she had ever felt safe or happy" (104). But with their conversation she felt sad to find that his ideas had changed: "He's changed, he's awfully changed" (106). When Marya had tried to explain to Stephan about her relationship with Heidler the argument made him so violent that he had "caught her by the shoulders and swung her side ways with all his force. As she fell, she struck her forehead against the edge of the table, crumpled up and lay still" (143). Her Stephan for whom she had patiently longed leaves her wounded perhaps to die. Home which she searched in England and Paris; security, which she sought from her relations, Stephan and Heidlers; happiness of which she dreamt from the beginning, are nothing more than an illusion. "There is in Marya a sense of a lost past which has been stolen from her, and it is this sense of loss and being plunged into a fearful and 'shallow world' that allows her to move from one circumstance to another finding protection from the shadows," observes Staley (40). But shadows aren't anything substantial providing only a temporary protection. Julia Martin like Marya had shifted from England to Paris. For ten years she had drifted away from her home where she had an ailing mother and a sister. When she returns walking around the London streets she felt that "her life had moved in a circle. Predestined, she had returned to her starting point in this little Bloomsbury bedroom [...] she had left nearly ten years before [...]. Perhaps the last ten years had been a dream; perhaps life, moving on for the rest of the world, had miraculously stood still for her" (67). Maybe time had 'stood still' for her but for rest of the things time has progressed. It had nourished antagonistic feeling in the hearts of her relatives. Her sister Norah looks at her "as if she were something out of the zoo" (73). But "she had been longing for some show of affection" (73) which was not reciprocated by her sister. Julia had taken care to dress up tidily because she thought they would be ashamed to see her shabby and would give her a cold shoulder. But even with all the pains that she takes she is not warmly received. Norah cuttingly says to her: "[...] I thought it very odd of you to turn up here at a moment's notice and to send for me and expect that I can produce money for you" (75). But it was not money for which she came to London. Uncle Griffith coldly tells her: "You always insisted on going your own way [...]. You deserted your family. And now you can't expect to walk back and be received with open arms" (84). Julia felt that the doors were slowly closing for her. Heavy at her heart she accepts the fact that it was idiotic for her to come: 'It's childish to imagine that anybody cares what happens to anybody else' (84). She goes to Acton to meet her mother: "She felt too nervous [...] supposing that her mother knew her or recognized her and with one word or glance put her outside [...] as every body else had done" (96). She knew if such a thing happened 'it would finish her; it would be an ultimate and final judgment' (96). But her mother had recognized her. For Julia her mother was 'the sweet, warm center of the world' (107). Her mother died shortly. Julia was 'tortured because her brain was making a huge effort to grapple with nothingness' (103). With her mothers death all the filial chords snapped. The man for whom she had abandoned her family had already deserted her. The home to which she longed to return ceased to exist. She had nowhere to go: "It was the darkness that got you [...] heavy darkness greasy and compelling. It made walls round you, and shut you in so that you felt you could not breathe. You wanted to beat at the darkness and shriek to be let out. And after a while you got used to it [...]. And then you stopped believing that there was anything else anywhere" (85). On the surface level it is Julia's constant search for money that is focused but there is a quest in the deeper level for some human engagement. She is a woman who had been isolated for long and yet is so depended that nearly every human contact seems doomed before it has begun. Her own past, broken relationships with her family and ill-fated affairs torment her. We "realize that Julia's journey is both forward and backward, but further discovery seems to lie in neither direction" (Staley 69). Anna Morgan, a Creole with her step-mother Hester comes to England. But her step-mother did not love or take care of her as she had promised. Her island home ceased to exist with her father's death and her mother sold Morgan's Rest, the beautiful house, under the impression that she required the money for Anna's upbringing. Anna begins to work as a chorus-girl in order to make her living. She meets Walter with whom she wants to build her lost home: "This is a beginning [...]. I'll go to all the lovely places I've ever dreamt of" (25). But this never happens. Their relationship soon ends. She aimlessly moves around London trying to make her living, dreaming to return to her island: "[...] drift, drift / [...] away from despair" (90). She longed for her native friend Francine: "she'll smile and [...]. I'll say Francine I've had such an awful dream—it was only a dream she'll say—and on the tray the blue cup and saucer and the silver tea pot so I'd know for certain that it had started again my lovely life [...]" (115). In England she felt vague and dislocated: "Her life in the islands, for all its richness, failed to prepare her for the harder, colder England. Her voyage is one of darkness, and one which seems to carry her further and further away from those vital qualities of life that seemed to exist in the Islands" (Staley 61). She could not get back the warmth and protection of the childhood that she had spent in the West Indies. Torn away from one she was unable to adapt herself to the other. Sasha Jansen in Part III recollects her marriage to Enno with whom she had come to Paris and then had broken up. With her marriage she felt that her misery would be over: "My beautiful life in front of me, opening out like a fan in my hand" (118). But she was beginning to grow tired thus waiting for happiness: "I look [...] too thin—and dirty and haggard, with that expression that you get in your eyes when you are very tired and everything is like a dream and you are starting to know what things are like underneath what people say they are [...]. I didn't think it would be like this" (121). All these culminate in Enno leaving her blaming her for passivity: "You don't know how to make love [...] you're too passive, you're lazy, you bore me" (128). Enno arrives again but things had changed. She gives birth to a stillborn child. Enno once more leaves. Nowhere to return she wonders in the Paris streets one after the other, and from room to room she moves: "Eat. Drink. Walk. March. Back to the hotel. To the Hotel of Arrival, the Hotel of Departure, the Hotel of the Future [...]. Back to the Hotel without a name in the street without a name. You press the button and the door opens. This is Hotel Without-a-Name in the street Without-a-Name, and the clients have no names, no faces. You go up the stairs. Always the same stairs, always the same room" (144-45). With her home being lost as if it is her identity, which has become blurred. She travels back to England but after some time she comes back to Paris for a change, she wants to forget her past, to begin everything anew which seems impossible. She journeys through 'dark streets, dark rivers, the struggle and the drowning [...]' (10) to be 'gradually sucked into the center, the dead center, where everything is stagnant, everything is calm' (44). After her broken marriage when Sasha had tried to return to her relations they spitefully reply: "We consider you as dead [...]. Why didn't you drown yourself in the Seine?" She reflects: "I have no pride—no pride, no name, no face, no country. I don't belong anywhere. Too sad, too sad [...]" (44). She further goes on with her monologue: "Yes, I am sad, sad as a circus-lioness, sad as an eagle without wings, sad as a violin with only one string and that one broken [...]" (45). As jungle is the proper home of a lion, powerful wings are a hawk's pride and a string produces the notes in a violin, it is love that helps one to live a life in happiness. This love is the attachment, the feeling of security and safety that one finds from one's own people, from a home filled with sacred warmth. But Sasha stands outside this sacred circle of warmth, they will not take her in. Antoinette spent her childhood in the Coulibri Estate in Jamaica. Though she was with her mother and brother she was a lonely child. Her brother was a sick child, a sickness from which he would never recover. So her mother could never attend to the daughter. When Antoinette went to her trying to soothe her she was "pushed [...] away, not roughly but calmly, coldly, without a word, as if she had decided once and for all that [...] [she] was useless to her" (5). She always longed to be with her mother: "[...] once I made excuses to be near her when she brushed her hair, a soft black cloak to cover me, hide me, keep me safe" (8). Later her mother married Mr. Mason. But some days later the natives set the estate on fire and her brother was badly burnt. He died. Out of grief her mother turned mad. Antoinette was sent to a convent. So from her very childhood she was starved from the want of affection. It was in the convent that she tried to identity herself with her other companions: "This convent was my refuge" (37). Antoinette was growing up and Mr. Mason wanted her to come and live with him and Aunt Cora. With this her life in the convent came to an end. Soon her half-brother Richard married her to an English gentleman. The marriage was only a business deal and her husband did not love her. He found her beautiful, mysterious and a stranger. He thought she had "long, sad, dark alien eyes" (46): "The girl is thought to be beautiful, she is beautiful. And yet […]" (49). But Antoinette loved him. He had given her life and happiness which she was afraid of losing: "[…] if one day you didn't wish it […] suppose you took this happiness away when I wasn't looking" (68). But his feeling for her was entirely different: "I did not love her. I was thirsty for her […]. I felt very little tenderness for her, she was a stranger to me […] who did not think or feel as I did" (69). Daniel Cosway who was Antoinette's half-brother from her father's side provides her husband a weapon to get rid of Antoinette. "There is madness in that family" (71) he informs him. He gets an excuse to blame and hates Antoinette all the more. Antoinette wants her husband to love her. She asks Christophine to help her with her magic potion as she practiced the obeah art. But their relationship broke. She had always felt alienated unable to identify herself with anyone: "[…] white cockroach. That's me. That's what they call all of us who were here before their own people in Africa sold them to the slave traders. And I've heard English women call us white niggers. So […] I often wonder who I am and where is my country and where do I belong and why was I ever born at all" (77). Her marriage wiped off her identity further as her husband would call her Bertha instead of Antoinette: "Bertha is not my name. You are trying to make me into some one else, calling me by another name" (115). Her husband purposely hurt her by getting physically involved with the maidservant Amèlie. This breaks her completely. Christophine was shrewd enough to guess all about it before hand. She had charged him: "You want her money but you don't want her. It is in your mind to pretend she is mad" (127). He was indeed cruel. Her had intoxicated her by pretending to love her making her love him in return. Then he withdrew, but she could not become practical and her desire was starved. He, erasing her identity, hastened the process of insanity. This is what love did to her: "She was only a ghost. A ghost in a gray daylight. Nothing left but hopelessness" (135); "the doll had a doll's voice, a breathless but curiously indifferent voice" (135); "[…] the doll's smile came back-nailed to her face" (136). She had dreamt that in England everything will change: "I will be a different person when I live in England and different things will happen to me […] England, rosy pink in the geography book map [...]. I know that house where I will be cold and not belonging [...]. In that bed I will dream the end of my dream" (84). And in England, which her husband calls 'home,' she is kept locked in an attic away from all the vital qualities and warm colours that surround the rest of the house. She dreams to fly away to her island with magical wings and this is the last of her dreams as she stealthily creeps out of the attic to give it shape. So in the novels of Rhys her protagonists journey in quest of homes that do not exist in their world. In the *Quartet* Marya's attempt is frustrated. Julia in *After Leaving Mr. Mackenzie* tries to make a return but is never accepted, Anna in *Voyage in the Dark* knows that her island lies oceans apart where she can never return, for Sasha in *Good Morning, Midnight* this home is nonexistent, and for Antoinette in *Wide Sargasso Sea* this home lies destroyed without a warm hearth or love to make her feel safe and happy. They are dispossessed women living in diaspora in an 'unhomely world' (Carr 63).

Rhys, a white Creole with a Welsh father, stepped into Europe when seventeen with memories, but the memories were perhaps not of roots, but of rootlessness. Again she leaves England for Dominica and on her return discovers to her dismay, that owing to her various experiences and changed perception of life, her home has ceased to exist. She discovers, in other words, that she has become an alien among her own countrymen. So while Odysseus gets back to his home in Ithaca, Rhys on the other hand lands in a state of homelessness in her official home. It is this paradigm of complex perception of life, which one can discover, inscribed in all her novels when viewed from different angles. She is a string and each protagonist a pearl. When stringed together a clear portrait of life magically becomes visible. Each protagonist has her own sad story to tell yet they stand at different stages of experience. A journey begins with inexperienced Marya who with her dreams safely wrapped up steps into the vile world. It scatters her dreams breaking her illusion. Julia unlike Marya is hardened by circumstance. She knew the rules of the game that Marya was innocent about. Though shattered at her heart she carefully dressed herself: "she made herself up elaborately and carefully [...] a mechanical process, partly a substitute for the mask she would have liked to wear. To stop making up would have been a confession of age and weariness. It would have meant that Mr. Mackenzie had finished her" (14). Julia accepts her position as a jilted mistress and is not ashamed of it. Anna although accepts her hopeless situation longs to get back to her Island home. Sasha is the only character of Rhys who has got some money and can ultimately realize all the dreams of buying new clothes the others had so long dreamt. She also becomes a temporary protector for a poor painter by buying a painting and thus helping him. She also acts as a protector for a gigolo. Antoinette is the most shattered and wiser of all the characters. She knew, once out of ones home there is no return, that death is the only way to achieve freedom, peace and happiness. And this is the measure she takes. So her heroines appear to be fragments out of her own broken self. Veronica Marie Gregg says in *Jean Rhys's Historical Imagination*: *Reading and Writing the Creole*: "There seems to be a wide range of interpretive opinions for an analysis of Jean Rhys's writing […]." In 1950 Francis Wyndham put forward the theory of the 'composite' heroine, observing that "essentially the novels deal with the same woman at [...] different stages of her career." So reading the novels of Rhys is like a voyage for the readers, a journey in the 'wide Sargasso sea,' drifting in the mindscape of the characters, beholding the lives of those who move around in quest of a home but ultimately achieve something much superior—freedom from the forces of society, which try to crush them. It may not be wrong to say that Rhys splits herself into the protagonists of her novels which, taken together, form, as it were an inverted *Odyssey*.

SELECT BIBLIOGRAPHY

Carr, Helen. *Jean Rhys*. United Kingdom: Northcote House Publishers, 1996.

Gregg, Veronica Marie. *Jean Rhys's Historical Imagination: Reading and Writing the Creole*. 24 July 2006 online <http://www.angelfire.com/com/hi/Jean Rhys/identity.html.

Rhys, Jean. *After Leaving Mr Mackenzie*. London: André Deutsch, 1969.

——. *Good Morning, Midnight.* London: André Deutsch, 1976.

——. *Quartet*. England: Penguin Books, 1973.

——. *Voyage in the Dark*. England: Penguin Books, 1969.

——. *Wide Sargasso Sea*. England: Essential Penguin, 1998.

Staley, Thomas F. *Jean Rhys*. London and Basingstoke: The Macmillan Press Ltd., 1979.

Locating Space, Identity: A Study of R.K. Narayan's *The Guide*

UJJWAL JANA

IN the contemporary context, the issues of space, identity and gender have constituted an integral part of postcolonial discourse. Quite inevitably, the concepts of home or homelessness, the individual self-exiled in a uprooted cultural space and battling hard for establishing identity find place in the migrant writings of such authors as V.S. Naipaul, Anita Desai, Bharati Mukherjee, Amitav Ghosh etc. R.K. Narayan's award-winning novel *The Guide*, which has been addressed from sociological, philosophical, ideological points of view, unerringly shows the scope for indulging in the issues of space, identity and gender. In this paper, I would like to elaborate the above mentioned issues in connection with a definite socio-cultural and patriarchal space.

In *The Guide*, the central character, Raju, is a scamp who ends up becoming a saint. For most part of his life, Raju exploited the emotional needs of other people, but the novel shows him going beyond the mundane concerns of earthly terra firma and being involved in quest for spiritual calmness and contentment. Raju's chequered life falls into three phases: his position as an enthusiastic and resourceful tourist guide, his love for and romance with Rosie and his inevitable fall, and finally his position as a spiritual guide.

A close reading of the text in the postcolonial perspective reveals that Narayan has portrayed the experience of the hero's (Raju) dislocation from his own home and simultaneously his search for identity to assert his individual self. Side by side, Narayan has dwelt on the issue of feminine identity in the figure of Rosie who can be looked upon as a rebel trying to carve out her own identity in a public space after being exiled from her own domestic space. The novel narrativises different complex circumstances with Raju moving from one direction to another to get his identity secured. But, this identity is in a flux and moves towards attainment of self-awareness. His quest for identity is tied up with the boundaries of home.

Raju starts as a humble shopkeeper, tending his father's shop at the outskirts of Malgudi. The beautiful natural and sylvan surrounding, at this stage, suits mapping out the cultural and psychological matrix of Raju's nature. His adherence to this 'home' at Malgudi gives him a sense of possession and belonging. Narayan quite deliberately makes a paradigmatic shift both in his home and identity. With the coming of railway to Malgudi, the original 'home' is gone giving place to new 'home' at the railway station. The cultural set up also assumes a new dimension at the railway station. From a naïve, humble figure, Raju becomes urbanized, seeking his identity as a resourceful tourist guide. At this stage, Raju is gradually dislocated from his cultural moorings. Things take a different turn when his romantic adventures with Rosie, Marco's wife, start. It is highly interesting to note that Raju violates all the ethics, decorum of a civilized society, comes in conflict with his mother, forces her to get exiled from her own 'home.' The text constantly plays with the idea of exile in different ways. Raju's identity also shifts. Raju the guide now becomes a manager for Rosie's commercial dance performances all over the country and comes into great affluence. Leaving aside his ancestral home Raju along with Rosie switches over to a 'stylish house at New Extension' which "was more in keeping with our status" (*The Guide* 186). It is very ironical that Raju's identity gets more and more complicated as the 'home' is shifted from one location to another. At this stage, a strained relationship develops not only between Raju and his widowed mother but also his neighbours. Thus Raju is exiled from his secured space of home. The 'stylish house at New Extension' also does not suit Raju's fate. In an act of forgery, Raju is exiled to a new home, that is 'Prison' and his identity is attuned to this new status—a prisoner. The novel not only chronicles the chequered career of Raju, but also reconstructs and reshapes the changing identity of Raju in the hybridized socio-cultural parameters. The idea of home and homelessness, alienation and marginalization figure prominently in this text. Raju's position as a prisoner accelerates his crisis of identity, his sense of alienation, and existentialist predicament. "Finally, after his release from prison, he literally and physically enters a strange, bewildering, and religious realm, when he takes refuge in the ruined temple on the river banks at Mangala" (Beatina 182). So Raju's final home at the ruined temple on the river banks at Mangala essentialises the process of transcendence on his part. His transformation into a spiritual Guru from a prisoner also corresponds to the locational shift from a prison cell to a temple on the bank of a river. Raju's new identity as a sadhu becomes possible only when he is posited outside the typical socio-cultural milieu. Raju's is a fluid identity which is reoriented and contextualized by the issues of possession and exile.

Narayan envelopes the feminine questions and gender problems "being positioned within patriarchal structures and threatened by male logocentrism" (Janic, 117). Here in this text, we have two female characters—Rosie and Raju's mother—who are projected as exiled and dislocated in a gendered discourse. Rosie who is born in a Devadasi family is a marginalized self in her own community. Her subjectivity and her identity is at stake at her own home and 'protected space.' She says:

> 'we are viewed as public women. We are not considered respectable; we are not considered civilised.' (*The Guide* 84)

Thus Narayan also harps on the issue of casteism and the social hicrarchy in which people belonging to lower caste are trapped up in a complex web and reduced to seclusion. In order to escape the stigma of her community, that is in quest of a separate identity, she marries Marco, a scholar, not out of love, but out of his social and intellectual status. Thus she is transferred to a new home to realize her aspirations as a dancer. In her new 'home,' she is once again subdued and marginalized. Alienation overtakes her with Marco dominating her and depriving her of essential self. From her position of a virgin to a married woman, she is found in the same state of existence. Thus marginalization of Rosie is also enacted in her husband's home where her attempts to establish an identity of her own are foiled and she is almost reduced to a chained figure. As a married woman, she tries to adjust with Marco as best as she could. But there was hardly any understanding between them. Often they quarrelled and she had to surrender to him begging apology. "But he gave her a cold look and returned to his work without a word." Rosie followed him, 'day after day, like a dog, waiting on his grace'; but he ignored her totally. Ultimately, she is deserted by Marco and takes her refuge at Raju's house. Thus Rosie experiences exile physically and psychologically and is forced to undergo the trauma of alienation within the society. By losing her position after the desertion, Rosie has to pocket insults at her new 'home.' She is seen in an awkward position as she being the wife of another man is forced to come to the discourse of patriarchy which paves way for her dependence on Raju. In her new home, she is a perfect stranger, and is in marginalized position as she goes against the codes of conduct of the Hindu family. Here, Rosie tries to establish her identity as a dancer so as to fill up the empty space, created as a result of familial relationship. She emerges as a promising dancer with her name changed. The more she earns fame and money the more the space between Rosie and Raju widens and the relation gets functional. Once again, she is exploited and used by Raju who commercializes her art. But she remains unbroken in spite of a number of hurdles. Struggling against odds since her childhood, she has learnt the art of how to cope up with male deceptiveness in a patriarchal social set up. Rosie, in this light, can be considered a representative figure of womanhood and a true embodiment of revolt against societal impediments.

Another figure in the text who is marginalized and alienated is Raju's mother. A typical Hindu widow, highly respectful of social values and ideals, she disapproves of Rosie's entry into her house. She tried her best to send Rosie away to her husband's place, but nothing worked out. In her own house, she is deprived of all her rights, and reduced to a poor figure. Moreover, she is rendered homeless and goes away with her brother in search of a new home.

The two figures—Rosie and Raju's mother—are no doubt ostracized in their respective homes, and pathetic victims to male chauvinism in patriarchal social set up. But, they represent two ideological standpoints. While Rosie reconstructs her own space, resists the reverse pull of male centred society and establishes her own self-identity on a strong pedestal, Raju's mother gets dislocated from her own stabilized position and fails to realize her own identity. If her gesture of leaving her own house is seen from a affirmative position, then it can signal as a silent protest not be bracketed within the fixed and sterile patriarchal social milieu.

WORKS CITED

Beatina, Mary. *R.K. Narayan*: *A Study in Transcendence* (U.M.I.300N.Zeeb Rd.Ann.Arbour, M148106, 1986).

Dengel-Janic, Ellen. "Exile as a Gendered Space in Anita Desai's *Fire on the Mountain*," *Journal of Literature and Aesthetics*, Vol. 4, Numbers 1&2, Jan.-Dec. 2004.

Narayan, R.K. *The Guide* (Indian Thought Publications, 53rd reprint, 2003) [All quotations in this paper are from this edition.]

❑❑❑

Of Continuities and Connections: Ramanujan's Translations

ANURADHA SINGH

FROM times immemorial, translation has played an important role in shaping the literature of the world. Glancing right back into the classical times, we find that literary Latin was greatly influenced by translations from Greek. In fact, the art of translation was practiced almost since 3000 BC.

The theories about the appropriate rules and principles of translation are as numerous as there are critics. Laborious discussions have been centre around such terms as "actual relationship" (between the source language and the target language), "factual replacement" (of the words of the original work—lexically, syntactically, idiomatically), and "the adequacy to the purpose." Questions have been raised as to whether or not a translation should use words from the original work, or whether or not it should imitate the style of the original. Opinions differ, too, about whether the translated work should be considered contemporary to the original one, or to the translation that is bound to be influenced by the other of his age and cultural milieu.

Total fidelity is, of course, a task near-impossible as no two verbal systems can exactly represent the same socio-cultural situation. There are such phonaesthetic barriers to be tackled as sentence balance, alliteration and assonance, and sound harmony. Rhetorical features such as meter, rhyme and onomatopoeia, to name only a few, add to the complexity of the translation process. Then, there are cultural obstacles to comprehension such as those posed by local metaphors, symbols and customs.

In support of the literary creativity of the translator Edward Fitzgerald, in his "Letter to Cowell,"[1] expresses the view that the translator is himself a creator who uses "a little art" to mould his literary works. Fitzgerald feels that the relationship between the translator and the author of the Source Language Text can be likened to that between the reader and the author, where the former retains the right to reinterpret and decipher the literary text.

Eugene Nida, a Bloomsfieldian linguist and a propagator of Chomsky's Transformational Grammar in his *Towards a Science of Translating*,[2] has made an invaluable contribution to the study of translations by advocating 'dynamic equivalence.' He is of the view that the fidelity of a translated work depends on how close the response of the target readership to the translation is to the response of the source readership to the original. Thus, the proximity of these two reader responses determines the adequacy of the translation.

The notions of the absolute separation between Source Language Text and Target Language Text, however, become all the more questionable, and the role of the translator as a creative artist even more prominent, when literature is viewed from Derrida's perspective. The famous deconstructionist feels that the term "original" is a misnomer, for there is already and always something else before that. Thus, no translated text can be accused of drawing from any original work. Rather, every original pleads to be translated. In this context, Gayatri Chakravorty Spivak writer in her *Preface to the Translation of Derrida's "Of Grammatology":*

> "Any act of reading is besieged and delivered by the precariousness of intertextuality. And translation is, after all, one version of intertextuality."[3]

This acute awareness of intertextuality leads the translator to recreate an "original" work, stylistically as well as thematically, in a way that would make it fit into his own cultural ambience. Thus, the effect of intertextuality, or rather the bearing of the translator's own age and socio-cultural conditions on the form, contents and design of the text has now been proven beyond contention. There has been a movement to see translation as a distinct literary genre. A system of analysis called the "Poly-system Theory" has been developed by Evan-Zohar.[4] According to this theory the divergence between the original and the translation is a significant contribution to the literary genre, and is in no way a distortion that demonstrates the defects of the translation.

This notion of literature as a poly-system, with individual literary systems as part of a whole, solves the conflict between majority cultures and minority cultures. It also comes as a welcome concept to diasporic writers who happen to be direct and acute victims of cultural conflicts and the dilemma of the translated self.

The parallels between a literary translator and a diasporic writer are many. Both need to sensitize to a number of cultural and literary options such as unusual collocations, unique traits of the languages under consideration and connotation factor. Thus, both are trans-creators, the endeavour of both involves intercultural mediations. This effort to strike a balance between two different poles in order to solve the question of authenticity is becoming more and more indispensable in the modern world of pluralistic identities, where there is a need to weave nations together, a need to promote inter-cultural bonding. B.K. Das rightly considers translational literature as "literature three"[5] written in the Target Language and based on the Source Language.

Translation, which has thus become a major source of intercultural study, is effectively used as a tool for bi-literary dialogue, self-definition and cultural identity by A.K. Ramanujan. That Ramanujan believed in literary as well as cultural translation is testified by his statement, "I am the hyphen in Indo-American."[6]

A careful review of relevant literature reveals that though much critical energy has already been expended on highlighting the exilic nature of Ramanujan's poetry, there is a dearth of studies which see him as a bridge between radically different cultures.

In fact, multiculturalism was Ramanujan's *fait accompli* from his very childhood. Right from his early days, he was accustomed to communicating in three different languages. With his father, Attipat Asuri Krishnawami, who was a professor of Mathematics at Mysore University, and also an astronomer, he conversed in English; with his mother, an orthodox Brahmin housewife widely read in Kannada and Tamil, he spoke in Tamil. When he went out of the house, he spoke in Kannada to the man on the street. Growing up in a house crammed with books in English, Kannada and Sanskrit, he was as well acquainted with astronomy as with stories from Shakespeare or other western classics.

With the plurality of his native culture deeply embedded in his consciousness, Ramanujan had an inherent inclination for cultural heterogeneity. Living in the U.S.A., miles away from his homeland, he neither suffered from the hyper-nostalgia detected in most expatriate writers, nor did he indulge in a mindless debunking of his roots which results from a blind infatuation of the dazzle of the western world. Contrarily, he had mastered the skill of walking the tight-rope between the two cultures that he inhabited. Thus, he had successfully put the problematic of his cultural ambivalence to rest by working out equilibrium between his past and his present.

Ramanujan had accepted his Indian roots as an inalienable part of himself, and therein lies the secret of his malleable cultural psyche. He did not sentimentalize or romanticize his Indianness as Parthasarathy did. Neither did he shun it totally like Moraes. He readily accepted its bearing upon his present. His past helped him to understand his present even better. Thus, for Ramanujan, his expatriate condition gave him the opportunity to keep up the dialogue between his past and his present, childhood and adulthood and between India and America without compromising on any of the polarities. His life and works exemplify this permeability of cultures, and nowhere is it more evident than in his translations. Ramanujan's translation into English from Tamil and Kannada could be considered as his attempt to see the two cultures he belonged to in terms of each other and decipher his amphi-lingual status. As he himself once says:

> It looks as if I lived between things all the time—two (or more) languages, two countries, two disciplines. My translations are a way to keep them all together.[7]

In 1960, when the South Asian Languages Programme at the University of Chicago included the study of Dravidian languages, William Bright, the well-known linguist, recommended Ramanujan to take the place of Ronald Asher, who was returning to the U.K. Although he did not consider Tamil to be his forte at that time, Ramanujan decided to take up the assignment. This half-hearted decision proved extremely fruitful as it became the genesis of his love for classical Tamil anthologies, and later led to his numerous works of translation.

Ramanujan started writing his poems in English and translating Kannada and Tamil poems almost simultaneously in the mid-1950s. In fact, the translations were interspersed with the publications of his English verse volumes. Among his translations, the significant ones are *The Interior Landscape: Love Poems from a Classical Tamil Anthology*[8] (1967), *Samskara: A Rite for a Dead Man*[9] (1976) by U.R. Ananthamurthy, *Poems of Love and War*[10] (1985), and *Folktales from India*[11] (1992). Besides, he has also translated and analyzed the text of the Virasaivas of Kannada in *Speaking of Siva*[12] (1973) and the Alvars of Tamil in *Hymns for the Drowning*[13] (1981). At the time of his death, he was working in collaboration with John Carman and Vasudha Narayanan on a more clarified version of these Tamil poems.

As in his English poems, in his translations too, Ramanujan sought for connections between different languages, texts, genres, literatures, historical periods and cultures. Aware that translation was not an easy job to accomplish, he chose to translate only the works from Tamil and Kannada—the two languages he knew well—into English.

As there is a gaping cultural gulf between Tamil and Kannada, and English, the same is between India and America. The task of bridging this cultural abyss, according to the poet, involves various hurdles quite akin to existential pangs. He says:

> [...] items are more difficult to translate than relations, textures more difficult than structures, words more difficult than phrasing, linear order more difficult than syntax, lines more difficult than pattern. (*Hymns for the Drowning,* xvi)

Speaking of Siva bears testimony to the fact that the most formative influence on Ramanujan was that of the Vacanakaras. This volume contains, in the words of the poet himself, "whatever struck me over the past four decades" (*Speaking for Siva*, 12). The Vacanakaras were Virashaivite saints who had raised their voices against the oppression of the poor, the low-class and the cut-caste, in order to reform Hinduism. They did not believe in religion as something inherent. In this matter, they were like the *Bhakti* saints. Like the Buddhists, they upheld *ahimsa* or non-violence towards all creation. Ramanujan's contemplation, at one point in his life, of embracing Buddhism, may be an outcome of the influence of these *Vacanakaras*.

As Ramanujan wrote his translations and his original English poems side by side, it is not surprising that his English poems have explicit hints of echoes from his translations. Many of his poems have a repetitive crescendo-like style, which also marks the *vacanas*. "Anxiety" (*Collected Poems of A.K. Ramanujan*, 29), and "Love 1: what she said?" (*Collected Poems of A.K. Ramanujan*, 219) are good examples of such climactic rhetorical effects. Again, like the *vacanas*, many of Ramanujan's English poetic pieces have a cyclic or sequential mode. A case in point is the poem "Elements of Composition" (*Collected Poems of A.K. Ramanujan*, 121-23) in *Second Sight*, fourteen parts of which have now become as many separate poems, Ramanujan exploits the conversational, candid tone of the *vacanas* in poems like "The Hindoo: he doesn't hurt a fly or a spider either" (*Collected Poems of A.K. Ramanujan*, 62-63). Numerous similes and images of Virashaivite poetry have been inculcated into his English poems by Ramanujan, the main ones being "the seed and the tree"; "the spider and the web" and "the dance and the sport." The image of the tree has been used by the *Vacana* poets like Basavanna, Mahadeviyakka and Allam Prabhu. Basavanna compares the relation between Lord Shiva and his devotees to that between the roots and the shoot of a tree. In Ramanujan's English poems, of course, it becomes the *Vamsa Vriksha*, or the family tree. Ramanujan, like the *vacanakaras*, who laid stress on the 'moving' (*jangama*) as opposed to the 'standing' (*sthavara*), can be said to propagate motion and continuity. He was of the conviction that a stasis in the cultural life of a person stagnates his inner being as well as his outer perceptibility. His translations can be interpreted as his endeavor to keep up the continuity and co-existence between his India past and American present, Ramanujan says:

> English and my disciplines (linguistics, anthropology) give me my 'outer' forms—linguistic, metrical, logical and other such ways of shaping experience; and my first thirty years in India, my frequent visits and field trips, my personal and professional preoccupations with Kannada, Tamil, the classics and folklore, give me my substance, many 'inner' forms, images and symbols. They are continuous with each other and I can no longer tell what comes from where.[14]

This concept of the 'inner' and 'outer' forms Ramanujan may well have adopted from Tamil *Sangam* (cankam) poetry which the poet has translated in *The Interior Landscape* and *Poems of Love and War*. *Sangam* poetry is broadly classified into *Akam* (inner) and *Puram* (outer) poems. While the former are lyrical, subjective love poems, the latter are more objective and comprise all kinds of poems on a variety of external events. It was Ramanujan's constant endeavor to amalgamate his inner and outer forms, both in poetry and in personal life. He has modelled his English poems on *Sangam* poetry and explicates the importance of doing so:

> The inner and outer are expressions of one another; the scene and the agent, each containing the other, are related in intimate metonymy.[15]

The Interior Landscape, of which *Fifteen Poems from a Classical Tamil Anthology*[16] forms an integral part, consists of translations of love poems from the classical Tamil anthology, *Kuruntokai*. Perhaps one of the earliest anthologies of classical Tamil poetry, *Kuruntakai* consists of dramatic monologues of the lover or the loved one. The poems are rich in figurative language and picturesque imagination. Ramanujan has translated these poems very effectively, keeping close to the meaning but altering it where his poetic art demands any such alteration. He has interspersed his translations with such classical words as '*kurinji*,' '*erukkam*' and '*konrai*' so as to retain the native flavour of the poems. This extra-ordinary work of translation won Ramanujan the Gold Medal of the Tamil Author's Guild in 1969. Prof. Iyengar has generously lauded the poet's art of translation and says that "it is no small achievement to have matched the old sophistication of romantic love to the current sophistication of linguistic finish."[17] Here is an apt example of Ramanujan's effective translation of classical Tamil into English:

> Certainly larger than earth,
> Higher than skies,
> more fathomable than the waters,
> is this love for this man
>   of the mountain—slopes
>   where the bees make rich honeys
>   from the flowers of the kurinji
>   that has such black stalks.[18]

Poems of Love and War is a mammoth volume of translations from four of the eight classical Tamil anthologies—*Kuruntokai, Narrinai, Akananuru, Ainkurunuru*. The volume is divided into four books—**Book I** consists of *Akam* poems, which are based on love and its various aspects; **Book II** contains *Puram* poems dealing with pieces on public events like war and the death of kings; **Book III** comprises of poems in a different key, or love poems in a comic mode; and **Book IV**, 'religious poems,' is drastically different in mood and matter from the three earlier books, and speaks poet's devotion to Lord Murukan (or Murugan). Through the translation of these Tamil poems, Ramanujan has succeeded in upholding admiration for Dravidian culture and literature to the entire English-speaking world. Of this volume of translation the poet himself says:

> These poems are 'classical,' i.e., early ancient; they are also 'classics,' i.e., works that have stood the test of time, the founding works of a

whole tradition. Not to know them is not to know a unique and major poetic achievement of Indian civilization. (*Poems of Love and War*, ix)

Ramanujan's urge to integrate opposites can be seen in the translation of Shrivaishmana Bhakti poems by Nammalvar, a tenth century Tamil poet devoted to Lord Vishnu, in *Hymns for the Drowning*. The *Bhakti* saints were great amalgamators who attempted to bring together the high and the low, the esoteric and the commonplace, the abstruse and the simple. Ramanujan observed this quality of bringing together the opposites in the *alvar* saints, too. In the "Afterword" to *Hymns for the Drowning*, Ramanujan designated their poetry as "the poetry of connections, of continuities" (*Hymns for the Drowning*, 166-67).

This volume contains a total of 83 poems, 76 from the *Tiruvamoli*, and 7 from the *Tiruviruttam*. Both the original volumes are by Nammalvar, and together comprise of about 1202 poems (1102 from *Tiruvamoli* and 100 from *Tiruviruttam*). Arranged in groups of ten, they have unity of metre, theme and diction. There are constant allusions in them to the Vishnu mythology which tells of various incarnations of the Lord as Vamana, the Boar, the Lion, and as Lord Krishna himself. Ramanujan's translation of these poems is enriched by his profound knowledge of the *Vedas*, the *Upanishads*, the *Puranas*, and the *Sangam* lyrics.

Besides Tamil poetry, Ramanujan has also translated a Kannada novella by Prof. U.R. Ananthamurthy, a writer of Gandhian ideology. The novella, *Samskara: A Rite for a Dead Man*, was written in 1965 and made into a movie in 1970. Ramanujan has said that "U.R. Ananthamurthy's *Samskara* is an important novel of the sixties. It is a religious novella about a decaying Brahmin colony in a Karnataka village, an allegory rich in realistic detail" (*Samskara: A Rite for a Dead Man*, viii). Ramanujan first published his translations of the novel serially in the columns of *The Illustrated Weekly of India* in 1976. The translator thinks that of the nine possible meanings of the word 'Samskara,' 'funeral obsequies,' suits the given context best. The story of the novel deals with the death of one Naranoppa which in turn leads to numerous deaths by plague. Moral degradation continues in the village until the birth of a man called Praneshacharya who is reborn as the dwij of Naranappa. Ramanujan has armed his translation with useful notes on Hindu myths, rituals and customs in order to make it self-contained and faithful, yet readable.

Ramanujan's life-long business to connect India and his foreign milieu continued in his translations of various folklores from India. The poet was greatly fascinated by the ability of these local tales to catch the attention of people of all ages and sexes. He saw the world of folktales as a counter point to the world of epics and mythologies which are constantly heard and translated. The poet's interest in folklore can be traced back to his childhood days in a traditional Hindu family. He reminisces how "cooks/ and grandmother/ had fed me rice/ and ages."[19] Much later in life, as a successful expatriate poet, this preoccupation with these age-old tales became a ramification of his nationalistic feeling and cultural concerns. Visiting India occasionally in search of these folktales, riddles and proverbs, he had realized that public as well as domestic culture remain unknown without a complete knowledge of folk idiom.

Perhaps the most culturally conscious of all post-Independence expatriate poets, Ramanujan's writings are abundant with his native moorings. His expatriation did not cause a discontinuity with his roots. Rather, he became extra-cognizant of his Indianness. He says in an interview with Chirantan Kulshreshtha that he refuses to consider himself as an exile or even an expatriate. On the contrary, his American surroundings make him increasingly comfortable with his Indian beliefs. The seepage of his Kannada and Tamil readings into his English poems highlight the fact that Ramanujan was fond of thinking of cultural interactions as osmosis instead of encounters.

REFERENCES

1. Edward Fitzgerald, "Letter to Cowell," 1951. Cited Rabindra Gargehs, "On Equivalence," *International Journal of Translation*, vol. 1, no. 1, Jan. 1989, 63-73.
2. E.A. Nida and C. Taber, *Towards a Science of Translating*, 1964 (Leiden: E.J. Brill).
3. Gayatri Chakravorty Spivak, tr. Of Grammatology, 1976 (Baltimore: The John Hopkins University Press), LXXXVI.
4. Evan Zohar, "Poly-system Theory" *Poetics Today*, 1979.
5. B.K. Das, *The Horizon of Translation Studies*, 1998 (New Delhi: Atlantic Publishers), 91.
6. C. Subba Rao, "Translation and the Language Syllabus," Tutun Mukherjee, 1998 (New Delhi: Prestige), 14.
7. A.K. Ramanujan, *The Collected Poems of A.K. Ramanujan,* ed. Vinay Dharwadker (New Delhi: Oxford University Press, 1995), 10.

8. A.K. Ramanujan, *The Interior Landscape: Love Poems from Classical Anthology* (Bloomington: Indiana University Press, 1976).
9. A.K. Ramanujan, *Samskara: A Rite for a Dead Man,* by U.R. Ananthamurthy (New Delhi: Oxford University Press, 1976).
10. A.K. Ramanujan, *Poems of Love and War from the Eight Anthologies and Long Poems of Classical Tamil* (New Delhi: Columbia University Press, 1985).
11. A.K. Ramanujan, *Folktales of India: A Selection of Oral Tales from Twenty Two Languages* (New Delhi: Pantheon, 1991).
12. A.K. Ramanujan, *Speaking of Siva* (Harmondsworth: Penguin, 1973).
13. A.K. Ramanujan, *Hymn for the Drowning: Poems for Vishnu by Nammalvar* (Princeton: Princeton University Press, 1981).
14. R. Parthasarathy, "How it Strikes a Contemporary: The Poetry of A.K. Ramanujan," *Literary Criterion,* 12. 2-3(1975): 197.
15. A.K. Ramanujan, "Parables and Commonplace," *Writers in East-West Encounter: New Cultural Bearings,* ed. Guy Amrithanayagam (London: Macmillan and Company, 1982), 141.
16. A.K. Ramanujan, *Fifteen Poems of Classical Tamil Anthology* (Calcutta: Writers' Workshop, 1965).
17. K.R. Srinivasa Iyenger, *Indian Writing in English,* 1962 (New Delhi: Sterling Publishers Pvt. Ltd., 1984), 671.
18. A.K. Ramanujan, "What She Said," *Fifteen Poems*, n.p.
19. Molly Daniels-Ramanujan and Keith Harrison, eds. *A.K. Ramanujan: Uncollected Poems and Prose* (New Delhi: Oxford University Press, 2000), 101.

Quest for Identity in Immigrant Sensibility: A Study of Bharati Mukherjee's *Desirable Daughters*

BHAGABAT NAYAK

IN the fluidity of global order the displaced person's quest for identity in the literary texts is greatly affected by the euphemisms of 'modernization,' 'westernization' and 'globalization.' The constant migrancy to the western world, in particular to America, reopens both "educative and creative" (Alam 48) values to the expatriates in their identities in Europe and America. Immigration is no more a motif among the migrants rather it has added new perspectives to their nation-state relations in the dangers of depersonalization and self-destruction. The fragile and fluid identity of Indian immigrants in a dozen American cities has become the theme of literary circles as they are neither nostalgic for their personal past nor afraid of the unfamiliar present, rather they try to escape from the dangers of depersonalization and self-destruction in the metaphor of Third World consciousness to the U.S. in their process of uprooting and re-rooting from unhousement to rehousement. In the quest for identity as an Asian-American woman Bharati Mukherjee (b. 1940) suffers from expatriate sensibility in her emotional self-distancing from India and adventuring in America. In her novels she gives much attention to the condition of Indian women immigrants in North America in the aspects of cultural collisions and in their control of their destiny. Like Anita Desai, Kamala Markandaya, Shashi Deshpande, Nayantara Sahgal, Ruth Prawer Jhabvala and Githa Hariharan, Mukherjee exposes many facets of feminism, encompassing agitation for equal opportunity, sexual autonomy and right to self-determination. Her earlier works had the complex weaving of colonialism, history and culture shocks but in her recent writings she has become more adventurous, more innovative and non-conformist like her literary counterparts, Salman Rushdie, Upamanyu Chatterjee and Amitav Ghosh. To her, immigration is a major motif and it is looked at from different perspectives relating to the issues of personal experience and the unhappiness in settling down and settling for the U.S.

The immigrants do not enjoy the life in "straight lines and smooth plains" and Mukherjee rather feels "very declasse" juxtaposing her characters who struggle in "a fragile identity and cultural hybridity to be preserved against obliteration" (Mukherjee 1986:3). Neither can she completely detach herself from her past nor do her characters have any certitude in the future. She focuses on the continuum of the immigrant experience moving from the small and the singular in the vastness of three time zones the past, the present and the future. The theme of identity in Mukherjee's novels in her Indo-American duality and personal dilemma is neurotic, schizophrenic, ambivalent and suspended between two worlds and rooted in neither. In the expatriate sensibility her woman protagonists think of India abroad in their bicultural perception, emotional transit and ghetto of nostalgia confronting multicultural society in the awareness of their social reality by carrying "core beliefs in the interior of the self against which all new experience is measured" (Lal 150).

Bharati Mukherjee declares herself an American writer of Bengali-Indian origin. She says, "I am an American writer, in the American mainstream, trying to extend it. This is a vitally important statement for me—I am not an Indian writer, not an exile, not an expatriate. I am an immigrant; my investment is in the American reality not the Indian" (qtd. in Naik and Narayan 108). She says, "For me it is a movement away from the aloofness of expatriation into the exuberance of immigration" (Mukherjee 1986:3). In an interview with Alison B. Carb she says, "My style has changed because I am becoming more Americanised with each passing year [...] I left India by choice to settle in the U.S. I have adopted this country as my home [...]. I view myself as an American author in the tradition of other American authors whose ancestors arrived in Ellis Island" (Carb 1990). In her Canadian experience immigrants were lost souls but in her transformation to a writer and a resident of the New World United States in the process of immigration is something different. Forgetting her Canadian experience as an expatriate, she is ready to welcome the freedom and liberty of America and frankly asserts that the immigrants should come out of their cocoons of defence into the openness of discussion. In her impression America has a culture of dreamers, and is a land of transformation and a cultural mosaic where an individual can reverse omens which is just what she did in America as she has reversed the omens of her Canadian experience. Like many post-colonial authors she craves for the identity of many Asian-American women who suffer owing to the complex issues of racism, sexism, violence, high social expectations and pressures, poverty, cultural adjustment, lack of family support, and post-traumatic stress disorders related to refugee experiences. Mukherjee writes about the actual condition of her characters in contemporary India and America which she sees through the lens of nostalgia as it is a quest for identity in immigrant, feminist and her existential sensibility deeply unravels her characters' awareness of the darkspots in their lives and their dauntless efforts to discover the areas of light. In her six novels, two non-fiction books and two collections of short stories, her protagonists are women and they confront a multicultural society in their emigration and evolution. Their displacement, alienation and search for the self constitute their quest for the institutions; 'home sweet home' and marriage that draws strength in their interpersonal relations. The protagonists have a quest for identity in their immigrant experience and move in the Yeatsean gyre of time to (re)construct and provide an organic unity to their life.

As Professor of English at the University of California Bharati Mukherjee is in close touch with female issues from the historical times to the contemporary society, and therefore presents in her novels the people who are "continually remaking their culture, and in so doing redefining the past, reconstituting the present and reconceptualising what they desire from the future" (Long 202). Mukherjee expresses her concern in contemporary themes, like quest for identity of immigrants in America's transnational and multicultural milieu for a materially better life and faces the tensions of adaptation and assimilation through the emotional and psychic syndromes. The issues of identification can be on many levels: psychological, sociological, linguistic, cultural and emotional, and the extent to which identification has been achieved on all these fronts will qualify how complete one's assimilation has been to the new surroundings. Her women protagonists are role models for several immigrant women in North America in their problems of falling in love, searching for freedom or establishing relationship. Transformation and migration are the two major issues of Mukherjee in her fictional world. Her characters are the victims of double civilizations in their migrated souls and they struggle in distant lands in search of fortune, some to fulfil their dreams and other in their quest for identity and stability in life. For four decades she has maintained her familial ties with her motherland, and continues to write about India and Indian immigrants to the west quite sensibly, consciously and conscientiously. In the postmodern climate the notion of America as a 'melting pot' of different cultures, ethnic identities and proletarian claims, presents migrants as economic refugees in their social displacements where their cultural and national identities struggle in cultural hybridity. Her struggle to identify herself with the new host-country enables her to write from a wider and more exciting angle. She understands that the new home, the host society to immigrants from many lands is a melting pot of multiculturalism where the expatriates become immigrants truly breaking the umbelical cord with their homeland. In her immigrant sensibility she thinks "immigrants are many times born and the assimilation is a spiritual rebirth, a recurring theme of Ms. Mukherjee's fiction" (Rao 271). Her immigrant characters are more Americanised and rooted in their adventure, risk and transformation and suffer from the insider/outsider syndrome in the individual's predicament of alienation, immigration, expatriation, exile and quest. Quest for identity is a postcolonial civilisational crisis in its centrality and an obsession. Physical dislocation has emphasised an identity in its historical and existential conjecture which is dealt with in the profane, immoral and impure multi-religious and multi-cultural context. In her search for the roots and authenticity of her migrant characters she creates the space of in-betweenness of different cultures, societies and homelands.

People become immigrants primarily for economic, political or religious reasons. America has become the nation of immigrants as the newcomers are offered the hope of a freer and more prosperous life. It is a great movement in demography in response to the factors, social, political and economic. In Mukherjee's fictional works diasporic identity is emphasised in immigrant sensibility. "Immigrants, refugees, exiles, nomads and the homeless also move in and out of these discourses as metaphors, tropes, and symbols but rarely as historically recognised producers of critical discourses themselves" (Kaplan 110). The immigrants suffer in their displacement but desire to return to their lost origins. The immigrant is represented as eager to reject that origin; "instead of a spiritual or creative identity and profession, the immigrant is associated with less romantic forms of labour—even, simply, with purely material motives, ranging from physical survival to elite careerism (ibidem). From her *The Tiger's Daughter* (1972) to *Desirable Daughters* (2002) one can observe a steady metamorphosis from acculturation to self-actualisation in Mukherjee's fictional works. In her earlier novels "identity and home are two intertwined issues often emphasised in her narrative telling of the mobility of the migrant subject" (Nyman 55). As the first naturalised American citizen to win much coveted National Book Critics Circle

Award for her *The Middlemen and Other Stories* (1988) she has come to the focus of attention for her recent novel *Desirable Daughters*. In the novel she deals with obsession as her favourite theme mingled with the issues of identity and collision of cultures that the exiles and immigrants face in the changed environment as they feel rootless and get dislocated.

The novel beginning with a traditional Brahmin Indian family in Bengal with three beautiful sisters—Padma, Parvati and Tara, acquires a meridian version of the Indian feminity. The sisters are brought up in strict conformity to the domestic customs and conventions of a conservative and traditional society with the values followed and preserved by the educated upper-middle class Bengalis. Padma, the eldest one is married to Harish Mehta, a non-Bengali business person and both are settled in Montclair, New Jersey with their grownup children. Parvati the pliable middle daughter lives in one of the expensive flats in Nariman Point, Mumbai with her rich businessman husband Aurobindo Banerji, an executive of a company. Tara the protagonist carries the name of her ancestors for whom her father chooses a perfect match, one Bill Gates—like Indian computer millionaire mogul Bishwapriya Chatterjee "the Icon of Silicon Valley" (Mukherjee 2003:274) the reigning genius hailing from an outstanding family. All the three sisters have got arranged marriages and they are settled in America and India. Tara and Bish settle down in Atherton, one of the earliest settlements of what later has come to be called the Silicon Valley, the site of civilizational plenitude. Bish's penchant to develop a system in computer technology called "CHATTY," a patented one heralds a major breakthrough in information technology that enables computers to route instantaneously urgent information in the least congested lines.

In the novel her women characters are the victims of double civilization in their fighting against the attrocities said to be predominantly male ethos. "Marriage and motherhood remain the main goal of a girl's life" (Rani 1994:106) and through this Mukherjee's protagonist establishes her identity. The story of Tara Chatterjee's trajectory from India to San Francisco and back to Mishtigunj (now in Bangladesh), the mythical site plays a major role in her family history and individual identity. The irony is that what was thought to be a very predictable, very successful marriage negotiation turns out to be a disastrous misbegotten marriage in Tara's life. Love in her childhood and adolescence was distinguishable from duty and obedience but now she realises:

> "Love" is a slippery word when both partners bring their own definition. Love, to Bish, is the residue of providing for parents and family, contributing to good causes and community charities, earning professional respect, and being recognised from hard work and honesty. Love is distinguishable from status and honors [...]. Love is having fun with someone, more fun with that person than with anyone else, over a longer haul. (*Desirable Daughters* 27)

Marriages in India are performed in parents' choice. A girl is given off in marriage to a groom completely unknown to her. She is taken to the marriage pandal like an embellished and attired goat taken to a deity for sacrifice. Tara expresses her dissatisfaction over this, and about her marriage with Bish she says, "I married a man I had never met, whose picture and biography and blood lines I approved of, because my father told me it was time to get married and this was the best husband on the market (26). In the first impression Bish was "the posterboy of Indian entrepreneurship" (26) very generous and protective to her but she realised him later as one for whom "Love was a spectrum upon which some men were old, like the Nehrus, Tagores and Subhas Boses, and some were slightly ridiculous, like Mahatma Gandhi, and some were exciting and unavailable like Jack and Bobby Kennedy, but others demanded closer scrutiny; they lay within a narrow zone of contention" (28). In her present status Bish is her old friend, ex-husband, a hopeless sexist and the surrogate father of Rabi. But she is well aware of the fact that her identity as an Indian wife in California is secured for Bish, the Stanford product, a promising electrical engineer, and discovers the big facts in America as he says "what you see is what's invisible" (49). Like many Indian immigrant women in their American status Tara has her frantic effort to seek, organise and affirm her identity and thinks how "in India, we didn't have outside influences [...] we didn't know family breakdown. Our families' inside is an impenetrable bubble. Anyone entering or existing was carefully monitored. We honoured the proprieties. There was no rebellion, no seeking after individual identity [...] we three sisters were treated with absolute equality, and we responded in total unanimity" (43-44). In her Americanised status Tara has a philosophical quest in the web of dualism. This disentangles her complex identity in an indiffernt city where she fails to surrender her personality nor is able to accept a new giant identity in the crisis of her life. She lives physically in immense advantages but enjoys a nomadic life in the cultural desert of America in her psychological invalidity.

Being fed up with overflowing superfluity in her life of opulence, Tara breaks all taboos and walks out of the wedlock with her son Rabi choosing a live-in relationship with a Hungarian Buddhist retrofitter, and doing volunteer work in a pre-school in San Francisco, all for her self-fulfilment. Her divorce is not known to her parents in India who like every parents desire their three daughters to be desirable for all time to them. But Tara with her identity as an 'oriental' American thrives on "That dusty identity [...] confidently labeled by father's religion (Hindu), caste (Brahmin), subcaste (Kulin), mother-tongue (Bengali), place of birth (Calcutta), formative region of ancestral origin (Mishtigunj, East Bengal), education (postgraduate and professional), and social attitudes (conservative)" (78). In California's Haight Street she has a different identity where she says "I am not the only blue-jeaned woman with a pashmina shawl around my shoulder [...]. All the same, I stand out, I'm convinced. I don't belong here, despite political leanings; I don't want to belong" (79). Tara's family are highly traditional and conventional and she has already a "sanitized upbringing." Her early affairs with Ronald Dey, a Christian boy, the brilliant brother of her friend Poppy was not liked by her parents as they advised her "if you sow the wrong kind of seed in the wrong kind of soil, you are bound to end up with an unhealthy sapling. That means no intercaste alliance" (107). She was happy to listen to the praise of her beauty and talent from her father's mouth; "no boy was good enough" for her. He was in search of some big shot businessman for her. But Tara is not ready now to accept Bish as a "sheltering tree" (in the words of Shashi Deshpande) nor she is complete ready to become a "breast giver" (in the words of Mahasweta Devi). In her subaltern and Third World marginality rather she appears like Mukherjee's Protean heroine in just braving the New World.

Tara's divorce to Bish and remarriage for rehousing with Andy is a transition in her life. She reestablishes her identity in immigrant sensibility and enjoys her life with Andy, a balding red bearded Hungarian Buddhist lover-contractor, yoga teacher, former biker and lover of Buddhist stories, haiku and kuan in a transcontinental society. In her double self she now realises Bish's super brain in retrospect and Andy's passion at present and in prospect. She considers Andy "a better father than Bish" (162) with whom she has now a different "sexual orientation" (164). During her Andy years she has become more American in the vicissitudes of her life and feels "beautiful enough, English speaking enough, Bengali enough, Brahmin enough, worldly enough and sophisticated enough, and still unknown?" and struggles enough in the story of each emigrant's life for identity. In immigrant sensibility Tara thinks of her Bengali identity like other Bengali "Armchair politicos and hot-air intellecutals" who feel proud of Satyajit and Tagore and they "have so much to be proud of" (182). When she faces the difficulties in San Francisco she blames her Daddy, Bish and Calcutta. But her son Rabi is a flawless American, not a perfect replica of his father Bish. Her loss and gain in the process of emigration has caused an emotional attachment to Atherton, her place of living that "grew like a baby" and she "felt a kind of maternal tenderness toward it" (260).

Quest for identity has the Darwinian dimension in the struggle of emigrants in American milieu. Tara thinks of the success of Bish and imagines how they have come from the same place; they share the same values, the same language and they share the two halves of one consciousness. After divorce in her assured feminine consciousness she raises question for Bish who perhaps forgets that "marriage is man's manifest dharma; his test, his duty, the outer sign of his inner strength and harmony" (266). Between her *patibrata* and *sati dharma*, emotion and emigration and American Brahmin and bohemian emigrant Tara thinks like her counterpart in *Jasmine* (1989) how she suffers from the nausea of disconnectedness, alienation and oppression of kinship. Remembering her past days with Bish to have brilliant children as "Calcutta couples have more time to go out together to lectures and plays" (249) she says "God created greed to protect us from too much spirituality" (267).

Tara describes her experiences from Calcutta and Bombay to San Francisco and New Jersey with her sisters. Conservative family background, convent education and superficial westernisation have provoked her quest for identity in expatriate sensibility. She thinks in nostalgia how the three sisters had more or less similar backgrounds and says, "sisters three are we [...] as like as blossoms on a tree" (21). Her mother had named them after goddesses to survive, prosper, and in order "to be Calcutta *bhadralok*, [...] share a tradition of leadership, of sensitivity, of achievement, refinement, and beauty that was the envy of the world. That was the legacy of the last generation of Calcutta high society, a world into which [...] three sisters were born and [...] have made [...] separate exists" (22). At nineteen when Tara graduated from Calcutta university with first class her parents had a desire to see her "a wife, a wearer of vermilion powder in her hair-part, not a widow, well into the age of white hair" (15). Tara's seven steps around the fire with Bish, ceremony of "*shubo-dristi*, the rite of auspicious gaze" (16) and her father's *gauri-daan*, the giving of virgin-bride-as-a gift" (15) had initiated her with a *mantra*, "a woman could attain nirvana only through worship of a husband" (19) remained a metaphor.

Padma, the eldest one, six years senior to Tara was beautiful and talented had won Miss Brains and Beauty for *Eve's Weekly*, had the ambition for some form of exhibitionism and anxiety to marry and settle in America. After her marriage with Harish Mehta she is now no more a simple upper-class Ballygunge girl; rather she has established her identity as a "multicultural performance artist" (94), a writer, a glitterati on the Indo-American television channels in New Jersey. In Padma's 25 years of staying in New Jersey her Indian bun hair style is not modified to an American beehive and her dress code is only restricted to saris, mehndi, henna decoration of the bridal hands. Her Indian identity is still expressed in the interior decoration of her house with "two framed Hindu devotional paintings decorated the walls" (203) and in wearing a dangling jhumka ear ring and a champakali necklace. She enjoys her life like that of the lords and ladies of Byzantium in the great city of joy. Parbati, the second one is married to Aurobindo Banerji and lives in Bombay at Nariman point with her two sons Bhupesh and Dinesh. The novelist assesses the three sisters as the "Youngest daughters are supposedly very trusting. Oldest daughters are innately suspicious. Middle daughters have a cynical optimism" (47). While Padma enjoys extra in family, more nervous, less expert and innately suspicious, Parbati in her middle order status is less assertive, cynical with optimism and more pliant than the former and latter. In comparison to them Tara is more special, relaxed and very trusting in her indulgence with her "Bengali beauty, wit, culture, athleticism and intelligence" (51). In the fluctuating current of innocence and paranoia in her odd family dynamics she says, "I'm bad at match, so I've settled on a simple formula for figuring out time differences between India and California" (52). She is a self-engrossed American with family connection in India. All the three sisters were proud of their perfect degree of worldly beauty, style, voice, manner and lord knows the provocation. Apart from their disparaged history, art and intellect, they were traditional Hindus and orthodox Bengali Brahmins with family nostalgia.

In the post-modern climate of the west the emigrants are quite well of but there is a persistent quest for identity in its genre and in their displacement. In their displacement and diverse experiences Homi Bhabha says: "the borders between home and world become confused; and, uncannily, private and the public become part of each other, forcing upon us a vision that is as dividing as it is disorientating" (Bhabha 1-18). Tara in her immigrant status has hyphenated herself with her native land though she feels insulated in the dilemma of being unable to return home and finding a home in the adopted land. She imbibes the best of Indian and western cultures through her struggle as a practitioner of feminist credo in which the social and legal aspects of ritual marriage are not central to one's existence in personal and social acceptance, but finds family to be an indispensable social institution. In India a wife's identity is part and parcel of her husband's identity but in San Francisco she finds "maintaining a healthy home life and respect for culture and tradition" (175) is the identity of a wife. Thinking herself as an archetypal immigrant she is in a bizarre obsession of grief between her emotion and reaction and in her cocooned Indian self and coddling American life.

Tara's quest for a happy home life is again disturbed by the appearance of one Christopher Dey the self-styled, self-appraised cousin of Tara, and Rabi's friend. By entering into the blissful world of Tara he claims to be the illegitimate son of her sister Padma and her one time lover Ronald Dey, presently a doctor married to Camilla Bhatt, a doctor from Ahmedabad. He apprises to her that he was brought up in a Catholic orphanage and has come to the states in search of his mother with a letter of introduction from her sister Parvati Banerji from Bombay. The unexpected appearance of her long lost nephew adds a delicate aspect to their Indian background. His disturbing disclosure about Padma's premarital motherhood and authenticity of the letter are questionable but she apprehends her sister's "conspiratorial" (124) relationship and its damaging impact on her reputation. The claim of this insolent stranger disorients Tara in her braving the New World. This opens up new dimensions in the story line leading to new revelations and it thickens the plot to be more complex. After Tara's enquiry of her sisters and Ronald Dey, Tara is confirmed that the imposter is a member of a cyber terrorist gang headed by Dawood, and intends to destroy Tara's ex-husband's worldwide communication network and destroy the prime targets high-techs in India and America through their crime network all over Asia and Middle East. When Tara's house is bombed by unknown persons it is suspected that the imposter Christopher Dey is Abbas Sattar Hai of Dawood Ibrahim's gang. The emergence and death of Christopher gives a twist to the plot by bringing a "smaller story inside the story" (277). Tara's final escape from the debris of her house, Bish's rescue of her and undergoing of plastic surgery add melodramatic effects to the plot. And all that Bish says with a philosophic resignation about the eventful night of house bombing was nothing but a confirmation from the gods of cosmic order that a segment of his life, his walking phase was over.

Unlike Mukherjee's, Tara's identity is involved in her agonised experiences, nostalgia and feminine sensibilities. Her experiences bring her to realise that wealth is a perishable commodity, the self, formed by inputs from this perishable commodity is equally perishable and big money invites big blackmail from big underworld. While Bish considers tradition as a centre-force of modernity, Tara constructs Indianness as a form of purity rather than as hybridity. In the cross-continental and cross-cultural dimensions the novelist emphasises the charisma of money as a thing beyond culture and geography. It is perceived that the search for self and identity come from the acquisitive drives of money where individual self is disturbed as "scandals smoulder behind the tradition-soaked, impregnable-seeming walls of upper class Indian family life" (Narasimhan 1). Further it appears that the beauty of three Bhattacharjee daughters is quantified but it is too much spiced with the scandal of unwed motherhood. Confessing her identity as an Indian daughter and American wife she says "The evidence of my virginity was soaking in the bath tub" (84). In the absurdities of American life she suffers from Sudden Freedom Syndrome (SFS) like many Asian American women who have only partial affiliations, disinterested identities and tactical belonging in their immigrant sensibilities. Identity and home are two intertwined issues emphasised in the fluidity of culture and social constructions of the narrative. In the words of Linda Mc Dowell "migration changes individual and group identities, affiliations and cultural attitudes and practices, among the mobile population of the 'hosts,'" (Mc Dowell 210). Mukherjee describes Tara as, "a self-appointed Joan of Arc" (221) and her problems as those of a liberated Indian feminine immigrant in her agonised involvement of never-ending quest for identity. She is proud to be brought up in a family in India where she had been westernised in "superficial, [...] convent school, metro cinema and movie magazines, which overlaid a profound and orthodox Hinduism" (178) and thinks "Divorce was not in our family vocabulary in the sixties" (101). In the

American milieu, silhouette life of Silicon Valley and her ex-husband's narcissistic projects she finds "It's all an illusion" (266).

The novel ends where it opens. The story of Tara Chatterjee's trajectory from India to San Francisco and back to Mishtigunj (now in Bangladesh), the mythical site plays a major role in her family history and individual identity. Tara travels to Bangladesh, her ancestral country; to Mishtigunj, a remote village where an ancestress bearing a variant of the name Tara, was married to a tree. In the year 1879, Tara, the five-year old girl was offered in marriage to a tree immediately after the bridegroom, a thirteen-year old boy died of snakebite. This superstitious marriage to a tree was done under the "full patriarchal authority over his beloved daughter" (11) is a watershed in the ancestress's life just like the blowing up of Tara's house in San Francisco and her miraculous survival. To this self-same village Tara, the thirtysix-year-old narrator returns 120 years later saddened if not wiser, with her Indo-American son Rabi to pay a visit to the tree-bride's home that unearths the buried colonnades of her consciousness, drawing a map of its archaeology. Remembering the saga of Ganguly family's last generation, Tara recollects child-bride Tara Lata's widowhood before her "happiest night [...] to become her lifetime imprisonment" (4). Tara Lata's bridegroom Satindranath Lahiri did not come, ululation, "shenai playing and dhol beating" (10-11) stopped and his father Surendranath accused Tara Lata's father Jai Krishna Gangooly for not appeasing and propitiating Manasa, the preventing goddess of snakebites that caused his family misfortune making Tara Lata a lady of 'hate and grief,' an "unmarriageable woman" (12) in her lifetime's virginity. Tara Lata's lifetime virginity with the tragedy of her husband's death was a force of her fortune for "selfless saintliness" (208). Tara, the narrator and protagonist narrates her ancestor's life as an inversion: "All of my life, or at least ever since my mother told me the story of Tara Lata the tree bride—and that I had been named for her—I have felt, for no discernible reason, a profound connection" (16).

The novel is written with evocative prose and read like a spythriller, a dose of cultural didactics and vernacular lessons. It is an Indian family saga with a difference, connected to a high voltage line of irony, disallowing the narrator (resembles the author in many ways) to take herself too seriously balancing between earnestness and self-ridicule. In its commonness Mukherjee uses the raw material that is available to every Indian expatriate writer—the immigrant experience, family relations, tradition, the sad spectacle of lives and internationalising the periphery. In her authorial voice and narratological technique Mukherjee has presented superbly, realised moments like the Brahminic culture and childhood memories in the texture of *Desirable Daughters*, with a fascinated nostalgia. In her orientalised glamour, socialite text, hybrid dialogue and multicultural metatext she has expressed the mundane qualities that are typical of the immigrant identity. In a review to *The Middleman in Midday* Bob Shacochis states that "Bharati Mukherjee has a genius for kidnapping our cultures then returning it to us, with a ruby in its ear, cardamom on its breath, gold threads, of syncretism, woven through its imagination." The novel is toned with excessive belongingness, homing-desire, mundane attitude, conflictual regionalism and dismemberment of the national myth. Quest for identity is a Third World concept in the post-colonial context that explores both history and values. The upbringing of "desirable daughters" is contrasted with the changing values of the new world they have come to embrace. Tara's quest for identity in the migrant society of the affluent Indians and multicultural landscape of global migrants reveals the spaces of tradition and fixed sense of identity of immigrant Indians in their situatedness. In Tara's realisation the novel reveals the spaces of tradition, personal memories, places and life styles, tradition and modernity, locales, nostalgic romanticisation of the past, and the inverted story of mobility, existential suffering, hybrid-subjectivity and plurality in her physical and psychic dividedness between rejection to the nativity and incapacity to deal with the new situation that makes the theme of identity more powerful and poignant in the mainstream of American life.

WORKS CITED

Alam, Fakrul. *Bharati Mukherjee*. New York: Twayne Publication, 1996.

Bhabha, Homi. *Location of Culture*. London: Routledge, 1994: 1-18.

Carb, Alison B. (Interview with Bharati Mukherjee) *Span* June 1990.

Lal, Malashri. *The Law of the Threshold*. Shimla: Indian Institute of Advanced Study, 1995.

Long, Elizabeth. *The American Dream and the Popular Novel*. London: Routledge and Kegan Paul, 1985.

Mc Dowell, Linda. *Gender, Identity and Place: Understanding Feminist Geographies*. Oxford: Polity, 1999.

Mukherjee, Bharati. *Desirable Daughters*. New Delhi: Rupa & Co., 2003 (All textual references are to this edition).

Mukherjee, Bharati. *Jasmine*. New Delhi: Viking, 1990.

——. (Intro.) *Darkness*. Ontario: Penguin, 1986.

Naik, M.K. and Shyamala A. Narayan (Quoted). *Indian English Literature 1980-2000: A Critical Survey*. Delhi: Pencraft International, 2001.

Narasimhan, Raji. "Moneyed Indians." *The Sunday Statesman Literary*. 4th May, 2003.

Nyman, Jopi. "Transnational Travel in Bharati Mukherjee's *Desirable Daughters*" *The Atlantic Literary Review*. Vol. 3 No. 4 (Oct-Dec) 2002.

Rani, Dharker. "Girl-wife-mother; The Marginalised in the Texts of Shashi Deshpande and Bharati Mukherjee." *Indian English Fiction 1980-90: An Assessment*. Ed. Nilufer E. Bharucha and Vilas Sarang. Delhi: B.R. Publishing Corporation, 1994.

Rao, P. Mallikarjuna. "Between Expatriation and Assimilation: A study of Bharati Mukherjee's *Jasmine*." *Indian Fiction of English*. Ed. P. Mallikarjuna Rao and M. Rajeshwar. New Delhi: Atlantic Publishers, 1999.

Shacochis, Bob. (Cited in review of *The Middleman*) *Midday*. Sept. 9th, 1988.

❑❑❑

An Irresistible Lure for Latin and Greek Roots in the Language of Science and Literature

DEVIKA

LANGUAGE, a natural human mental growth, flows in continuity that never ceases but remains in a perpetual state of flux. It can be the bearer of all kinds of truth and the imager of every sort of reality. This universal medium of conveying feelings and facts describes truth in different garbs. Language can be viewed from different perspectives: the language of masses, the language of aristocracy, the language of diplomacy, the language of law, the language of literature, the language of science and technology, etc. In every sphere of life, the need for a medium is there and that medium is language, which is comprised of befitting words. Words, the primary vehicles of thoughts may be related to something mellifluous or arid, depending upon the need of the hour. The language of literature cannot substitute the language of science simply because every word denotes something special.

Language can be *emotive* as well as *indicative* depending upon the standpoint. *Indicative* is used to state facts and *emotive* is used to arouse feelings or suggest an emotional attitude. The following sentences will exemplify the statement. If it is written, "There is a snake in the grass," it simply means a reptile, whereas if it is written, "What a snake he is!" it means the fellow is treacherous and can do harm. The first sentence is an example of indicative use of language and the second sentence is an example of emotive use of language. Indicative use of language is more apposite for the language of science and technology and emotive use of language goes well with the language of literature.

English did not use to be the way it is now; it has undergone a tremendous alteration. Initially it was not as rich as it is at present. Various conquests have shaped it in its present shape. In the first phase, that is, Old English it has been in its raw form, getting moulded in Middle English and Modern English period. It has become widespread as it gives admission to the words from various languages. Since English is a language that is a very rich amalgamation of words culled form the languages of all the corners of world with the preponderance of Greek and Latin words, Greek and Latin words form the basis of English language. In short, the words of Greek and Latin origin exercise enviable supremacy in English language, be it the language of science and technology or the language of literature.

Words are borrowed and used in literature and science and technology irrespective of being Latin or Greek. In the language of science and technology they are more to the point and crisp, whereas in the language of literature they are more symbolic giving way to subtle nuances that is something entirely different from the informative trend of scientific lore. The words of literature have different criteria for perfection and suitability. Words of literature should be spanking new, fresh, and inimitable in themselves; they have their own beauty in the sense of melody and music. Words like breeze, affiliation, aroma, galaxy, etc. have their own charm that can never be found in words like *chrysanthemum* (gold), *opisthocoelous* (backwards), *mesembryanthemun* (noon), etc.

The literary writer makes use of words which are quite mellifluous and intoxicating whereas the aim of the scientist is not to provide musical rhythm but to state facts in stark nudity or to put it otherwise scientist wishes for perfection in the sense that whatever he has to convey should have only one meaning to all the people throughout the globe irrespective of their region. Words like *psammophilous* (related to sand), *pneumotaxis* (related to breath), *aphrosiderite* (related to foam), *nyctanthous* (related to night) have respectively something to do with sand, breath, foam, and night; and they mean the same thing to people in India, Japan, Australia, or Great Britain.

Words of science are seldom attractive in themselves; for example, *hybrotropism* are certain spiders that prefer moist air to the dry one, and *chemotactic* are the senses of animals that seem to taste and smell with the help of organs on their legs. These types of words may be very useful and inevitable but they are arid and also leave the readers dry and panting for something fresh and bright. Euphony of words is nowhere to be seen in the words of science and technology as they have different purpose and utilization.

Since developments have been rapidly pouring in, scientists turn to their favourite Greek and Latin to find a word for labeling. An interesting thing to note is that literary writers have also derived from the same languages. The only difference is that they look for different qualities in the words of same root. Examples are galore. The root, which means yellow, forms word like *xanthoderma* (Gk), which means having yellow skin; not only this it is also used in *xanthic flower* in literature which means a person of everlasting beauty. *Catadromous* (Gk) means migrating down a river to the sea to spawn in contrast to *catastrophe*, which means a final event or conclusion, usually an unfortunate one along with other shades also. Similarly *syndrome* (Gk) and *sympathy* though they come from the same root *syn* or *sym* (which mean with) conjure the images of two different worlds.

The hunters of the words sometimes have taken words from both the languages and used them accordingly. *Ge* (Gk) means earth that is used in very commonly known words like *geology, geography* and *George*. Its Latin equivalent *Terra* is also dragged in words like *terrestrial, terrain*, and *Mediterranean*. The words from both the languages are used quite often in suitable contexts. Similarly the roots of the word *snow* have been taken and used from both the languages, e.g., *chionophobia* (Gk) means the *fear of snow* and *niveous* (Lt) means anything that *resembles snow*. The root words of moon in Gk and Lt, i.e., *selene* and *luna* create words like *selenography* and *lunar*. *Selenography* is the branch of astronomy that deals with the physical characteristics of the moon, especially with the nature and origin of its surface features. *Lunar* means *of or pertaining to the moon*.

In Greek *meta* means after and in Latin *post* means after and the words of both these combinations are used in literature and science. In literature *metamorphosis* is used to show *complete change of form, structure, or substance*, as transformation by magic or witchcraft. This complete change in appearance, character, circumstances, etc. is entirely different from *the metamorphosis of tadpoles into frogs* which is a change or successive changes of form during the post embryonic or embryonic growth of an animal by which it is adapted to a new or special environment or way of living. This word got so much recognition within and outside the ambit of science that German scholar Franz Kafka named one of his short stories as *The Metamorphosis*. On the other hand, *postmortem* a medical term meaning—of, pertaining, or occurring in the time following death—is also used as *a postmortem criticism of television show.*

Greek word *opisthenar* is anatomical word meaning *the back of the hand* and *opisthograph* means a *manuscript, parchment, or book having writing on both sides of the leaves*. This backwards or behind is used in Latin as *retro* making words like *retrospect* meaning *to look back in thought* when poets, writers are left with nothing to look forward to, then they look backwards. Greek *cata* (down) makes *catastrophe* leading to another similar word *cataclysm* meaning *a sudden and violent physical action producing changes in the earth's surface* in Physics and Geography and *any violent upheaval, esp. one of a social or political nature* in general. In Latin this downwards process starts with *de* and ends in the construction of words like *descend* meaning *tumble down* or *go down*. Whatever the meaning of *descend* may be its position has always remained steady in the pale of literature and used none can challenge it. It is also used with undisputable ease in the field of arithmetic.

It's not that the words are always so dissimilar that no guesses could be made for alikeness; some words are there that despite coming from different language roots are quite similar and give the impression of similarity. Such examples are *tria* in Greek and *tres* (meaning three) resulting in the formation of words like *triad* and *trellis* respectively. *Trellis* is *a framework or structure of latticework used as a support for growing vines, climbing plants, etc. woven with three threads. Triad* also includes the use of number three in all its shades, be it—*a group of three, esp. of three closely related or associated or an element, atom, or group having a valence of three or a chord of three tones* in music. Same is the case with *octo* that means eight in both Greek as well as Latin. *Octopus* means *a sea animal of eight legs* whereas *octave* means *a series or group of eight* in any field but both mean something related to eight; and it is to be kept in mind that *octopus* is a Greek word and *octave* is a Latin word. This trend is also very deceptive, as all the numbers don't follow the trend of similarity. A period of thousand is known by two different names such as *chiliad* (Greek) and *millennium* (Latin) because in Greek *chilioi* means thousand and in Latin *mille* means thousand, hence two different names for the same word.

Octopus and *octave* are strikingly alike and also refer to something related to figure eight still the words belong to different areas. *Octopus* is strictly related to the field of zoology whereas *octave* is a ubiquitous word in the arena of literature. This term exercises a specific position in the field of music and poetry. Similarly *trellis* belongs to the world of delicate ladies like Belinda, and *triad* as such knows no boundaries. It can slither in any field where something has to be done with figure three. Likewise *millennium* is a nychthemeron word used every time whenever the need arises for this figure in any of the fields. And same is the case with chiliad though in this form it's rather taxing to find its real meaning as this word has undergone a change in the form of spelling and nowadays we are acquainted with this root as *kilo* making familiar word combinations like *kilowatt*, *kilometer*, etc.

When we have multiple ramifications of the same word it means that in any of the languages more than one root corresponds to the various numbers of the same word. The glaring examples are the root words of *breath* and *rock*. In Greek *pneuma* and *pnoe* form the base for the formation of words like *pneumography* and *apn(o)ea* meaning respectively *the process of recording the movements of the thorax in respiration* and *temporary suspension of respiration*. In Latin *halitus*, *spiritu* and *anima* are the roots for words like *halitosis* and *spirograph*, which mean *bad breath*, and *an instrument for recording respiratory movements*. For rock in Greek there is only one root and that is *petra* resulting in words like *petrify*, *petrology* and *pertichor* which mean *turn into stone, the scientific study of rocks,* and *the fresh smell of earth (rocks) when first rain drops fall on the surface of earth*. In Latin there are three offshoots of rock, that is, *lapis, saxo* and *rupe*. *Lapidary* is a *workman who cuts, polishes, and engraves precious stones*; it also means *the art of cutting, polishing, and engraving precious stones,* and *an old book on the lore of gems*. *Saxatile* means *living or growing on or among rocks*, and words like *rupestrine* is also related to rocks. It brought into vogue various shades of the same word; it also justifies the use of a word into one particular region and then it also justifies the interchangeability of various words but with some shade varying.

The Greek words related to breath like *pneumonia* are known to even common people and when this suffix *pneuma-* appears rough guesswork can be made about its relation to breath problems but another root is strictly related to the ambit of medicine and is not known outside and this justifies the strangeness of words like *apn(o)ea*. Similar kind of trend can't be observed with Latin words related to breath. Latin equivalents are still strange to the ears of masses. Even today words like *halitosis* and *spirograph* move in the circle of medical professionals. The root of rock exercises a very rocky position; Greek root is known in various words like *petrify, petrology* and *petrichor*. *Petrify* requires no straining of brain for understanding but *petrology* is sometimes befuddling because of its association with word like petrol with which in reality it has no connection. *Petrichor* is also new in the field but once the root clicks it's not difficult to guess its meaning but it will take time to become common; right now it is more of a specific word. Only time will tell whether it becomes as common as *petrify* or not. Latin roots of rock are like rocks and don't show any inclination of coming out of the area to which they belong. That's why we see very little of them and whenever words like *lapidary, saxatile* and *rupestrine* appear they sound strange to ears.

It's not the case that a word is taken from both the languages. Certain words are there which have come into English from only one language and there is no equivalent from another language, and it could be either a Greek or a Latin word. The equivalent of English word *thunderbolt* has been taken only from Greek and the words that have sprung from *ceraunos* (thunderbolt) are *ceraunoscope* and *ceraunics*. The equivalent words of *picture* are taken only from Latin; the roots are *tabula* and *pictura* and the words are *tabulate* and *picture*. *Gate* takes Greek roots like pyle and pyloma and the resultant words are *pylorus* and *pylome* meaning *the opening between the stomach and the duodenam of the intestine* which literally means 'gate keeper.' For *punishment* we can refer only to Latin roots such as *poena, castigatione,* and *vindicta*. The ensuing words are *penalty, castigate* and *vindictive* meaning punishment in different garbs.

Words like *picture* mean only one thing in science whereas even this word coruscates varying shade in the field of literature. It's not the process of taking still pictures on a hard paper but it could be picture of perfection, poverty, beauty as well as dreams, a thing never dreamt of in science. Words like *penalty, castigate* and *vindictive* though they stem from the different roots are somewhat similar and somewhat dissimilar. *Penalty* could be legal, moral, spiritual, economical, etc. *Castigate* may mean reprimand, chastise, criticize, rebuke, scold, tell off, etc. but after certain digressions all shades lead to some sort of punishment. *Vindictive* is not far behind in this race.

To reprise, these words are used by human beings for their convenience to convey their ideas accordingly; when they feel that under certain circumstances they cannot do with one shade of meaning, they grope backwards for other similar words of diversity in rich languages like Greek and Latin. Literature people require various shades and subtle nuances of words to give an outlet to their view regarding life and its affairs that are quite elusive; that's why they ferret out multidimensional words. Scientists, on the other hand, need words which may mean the same thing to people all over the world because their aim to share the information of their findings and they wish people to understand the words only in the context which is the most apposite one. Hence, the needs and aims of both literature literati and scientists vary and so does their selection and meaning of words. They have never hesitated and will never hesitate to borrow from Greek and Latin, as both the languages are rich repertoire of befitting words.

BIBLIOGRAPHY

Greenough, James Bradstreet and George Lyman Kiltredge. *Words and their ways in English Speech*. Boston: Beacon Press, 1964.

Halliday, M.A.K. and Ruquiya Hasan. *Cohesion in English*. London: Longman Group Ltd., 1976.

Hogben, Lancelot. *The Vocabulary of Science*. London: Richard Clay Ltd., 1969.

Lewis, Norman. *Word Power Made Easy*. New Delhi: Goylsaab Publishers & Distributors, 1991.

Lindberg, Christine A. Ed. *The Oxford American Thesaurus of Current English*. New York: Oxford University Press, 1999.

Meadows, A.J. *Communication in Science*. London: Butterworths, 1974.

Savory, Theodore H. *The Language of Science*. London: Andre Deutsch, 1967.

Webster's Encyclopedic Unabridged Dictionary of the English Language. New Jersey: Gramercy Books, 1994.

Wrenn, C.L. *The English Language*. London: The English Language Book Society and Methuen and Co. Ltd., 1964.

❑❑❑